BRENDA GAYLE

Twice & Forever

Seasons of Love – Autumn

Twice & Forever
Seasons of Love - Autumn
by Brenda Gayle
Published Internationally by Bowstring Books
Ottawa, Ontario, Canada

Previously published by Lachesis Publishing Inc. as *Twice & Forever* (in *Love & Hope*) ©2016 Brenda G Heald
Re-edited & re-published as *Twice & Forever (Seasons of Love - Autumn)* ©2025 Brenda G Heald

All rights reserved. The use of any part of this publication reproduced, transmitted in any form or by any means, electronic, mechanical, photocopying, recording, or otherwise, without the prior written consent of the author, Brenda Gayle, is an infringement of the copyright law.

EBOOK ISBN: 978-1-7387434-5-2
PRINT ISBN: 978-1-7387434-6-9
LARGE PRINT ISBN: 978-1-7387434-7-6

This is a work of fiction. Names, characters, places and incidents are either the product of the author's imagination or are used fictitiously, and any resemblance to any person or persons, living or dead, events or locales is entirely coincidental.

To Bruce, whose love and support sustain me, and whose humorous anecdotes keep me—and I hope you—entertained.

ONE

Rain pelted the windshield making it difficult to see despite the rapid clearing of the car's wiper blades. The brake lights flashed on the vehicle ahead and the car swerved. Something rolled out from underneath it. Jill Bennett glanced up at her rear-view mirror—no one behind her—then brought her sedan to a quick stop a few yards beyond the thing crawling along the highway's shoulder.

"Jerk!" she muttered at the taillights disappearing around a curve. *Didn't even stop to see what he hit.*

She pulled up the collar of her trench coat—regretting that she hadn't taken the extra few minutes to attach the hood before she'd left this morning; turned on the hazard lights, collected a blanket from the trunk, and went to the rescue.

The animal hissed as Jill approached it. Its already cloudy eyes glared at her from a bandit's mask.

"It's okay, I'm here to help you." Jill crouched down and inched her way toward the raccoon. One of its legs was broken. She wasn't sure about the rest of it. There didn't seem to be a lot of blood.

That's good, isn't it?

She dropped the heavy wool blanket over the animal and counted to five as it writhed and screeched underneath. Then, as carefully as she could manage, she scooped up the bundle, turned it over so she could grab the edges of the blanket, and carried it back to her car.

Okay, now what?

Jill hesitated, the front passenger door open. She shouldn't put it beside her. Suppose it lashed out at her and she veered off the road? A cage would be good. She really needed to pick up a cage. The raccoon's frantic movements had stopped and her heart broke with each pathetic mewling. It needed medical attention—quickly. *Back seat, it is.*

Several cars had slowed as they passed her on the two-lane highway, but none had bothered stopping to see if she needed help. You'd have thought that a woman, alone, by the side of the road, in the pouring rain, might have warranted some gallantry. She sighed. *Yeah, maybe once upon a time, but not in this century.*

Jill started the engine and eased back onto the highway. It was just after five p.m., according to the illuminated dashboard display. Dr. Vanderhorst, her usual vet, finished at five. Chances were she'd still be there. The office was only about ten minutes away. But with this rain…

Dr. Palmer was closer. Jill didn't know him, but her daughter, Rachel, had got a job at his clinic the month before, based on her friend Mae's recommendation. And he was open late today. She'd learned that when she'd tried to rouse Rachel out of bed this morning and was haughtily informed that she didn't have to start work until noon.

Jill smiled at the memory. Rachel had never been a morning person. All through her teenage years, it had been a challenge to get her up and out the door in time for school. It still was. Odd how something that had caused her so much consternation in the past now brought a sense of comfort. Relief even. It was familiar. Safe.

Jill's return to work today was supposed to be familiar, too. But instead of resuming her position as an educational assistant at the local elementary school, a quick five-minute walk from her St. Thomas home, she'd been assigned to a different school, out in the country. True, it was only a fifteen-minute drive away, but still…

She shouldn't complain. The school board had been under no obligation to take her back. After all, two years ago she'd retired—well, quit, because she hadn't reached the proper age to officially qualify for retirement.

Was it two years ago? It felt longer. It felt like yesterday.

Jill flinched as a pick-up truck roared passed her and then jammed on its breaks as it cut back into her lane. She wasn't going *that* much below the speed limit. She was being cautious; the roads were slick.

She slowed at the traffic light and then turned right on Talbot Road. Dr. Palmer's office was just a few blocks away. The raccoon was quiet now. She glanced over her shoulder. He wasn't moving, either.

She made a quick left, turning south on the cross-street, at a Tim Horton's coffee shop, as Rachel had told her, straight through one stop sign, and then right into a small parking lot containing a half-dozen or so vehicles.

I hope he's not too busy. This was an emergency, but Jill hated the thought of delaying treatment to other animals that may also need urgent care.

As soon as she picked up the blanket, the raccoon made a half-hearted attempt to struggle, which she took as a positive sign. "You're going to be okay, Rocky," she said. The name seemed a good fit. "I'm going to make sure you're all right."

The receptionist, a Kathy Bates in *Misery* lookalike, didn't bother to hide her indifference as Jill introduced herself as Rachel's mother and explained why she was there. And had she really seen the woman roll her eyes just before she turned to lead Jill and her soggy bundle into one of the small examining rooms? She'd expected more empathy from someone who worked in a place that helped those who couldn't help themselves.

"Mom?"

"Hi, baby." Jill moved to hug her daughter but hesitated as she remembered she was still holding the blanket containing the raccoon. She glanced down at it, dismayed to see an expanding ruddy brown patch staining the fabric. *Oh no!* And on the floor, diluted red droplets of water and blood. *This can't be good.*

"You're drenched!"

Jill raised her free hand to her hair and tried to smooth out the tangled mess. She knew she must look a fright. She'd wanted to make a good impression her first day back at work, so she'd spent an extravagant amount of money on some new clothes and having her hair highlighted and cut shoulder length—similar to Rachel's, or at least how it had been before…

People always commented on how much she and Rachel looked alike: dark auburn hair and fair skin. But not their eyes. Jill's eyes were amber while her daughter had Calvin's deep brown eyes. And like her father's, Rachel's eyes could never mask what she was thinking, and what she was evidently thinking, right now, was that she was not happy to see her mother.

"It's pouring rain," Jill said in her defence. "Here, come help me." She hoisted the bundle up onto the metal examination table.

Rachel sighed, exasperated, and helped peel back the blanket. "It's a raccoon!"

"Of course, it's a raccoon. What did you think it was?" Jill hung on to the edge of the blanket, prepared to grab Rocky if he tried to escape. He didn't move, but she could see his chest rise and fall, proving he was still alive. *Thank goodness.*

"I don't know. I thought it was another dog or something. Jeez, Mom. A raccoon? What were you thinking?"

"Ladies?"

Jill's lips parted at the sight of the doctor. He was much younger than she'd expected. Her friend, Mae, had told her Grant Palmer had been her veterinarian for years, so she'd assumed he'd be in his sixties, closer in age to septuagenarian Mae. This man didn't look to be much over forty. His eyes were strikingly blue, and his hair was thick and brown—worn a little long for someone who was supposed to be a professional—and showed no sign of gray. His square face was clean-shaven, revealing high cheekbones and a pronounced jawline. A white lab coat hung open over a Toronto Blue Jays T-shirt, which was stretched taut over a broad, well-muscled chest and abdomen. And he was wearing blue jeans. She'd been giving Rachel a hard time about her casual clothing ever since she'd started at the clinic, last week. Maybe she should ease up on that.

"Dr. Grant Palmer, this is my mother, Jill Bennett," Rachel said.

"Pleasure to meet you, Mrs. Bennett. We're very happy Rachel's joined us. She's a terrific asset to the team." Dr. Palmer's large hand firmly engulfed hers. He wasn't as tall as she'd first thought—definitely not six feet; more like five-ten. At five-ten herself, Jill noticed height. Calvin had been shorter than her by an inch—no more than that—but sometimes that inch had felt like a foot. Dr. Palmer wouldn't have the same qualms about his height—he oozed self-confidence. "Now, let's see what we've got here."

He pulled on a pair of gloves and gently—but too briefly—examined the raccoon. He sighed heavily and looked up. "I'm sorry Mrs. Bennett—"

"Sorry? What do you mean 'sorry'? You've barely looked at him." Jill stepped toward the table, prepared to protect Rocky from what she feared he was about to suggest.

"His prognosis isn't good." He held up his hand, stopping her from commenting while he continued. "I can either put him out of his misery now or wait for him to expire naturally. I don't think it will be too long."

"You can't let him die. There's got to be *something* you can do."

"Mom!"

"Mrs. Bennett, I realize that you may feel some responsibility for hitting the animal—"

"I didn't hit Rocky. I *saved* him. The other driver didn't even slow down to see what he'd run over."

"Oh my God, Mom, you *named* it?"

"Regardless of the circumstances," Dr. Palmer interjected, "there is too much damage to his internal organs. The best thing we can do for him is to ease his passage as quickly and humanely as possible."

"Can't you operate? You can't just give up on him."

"Mrs. Bennett…"

Dr. Palmer's constant use of her name, and the exaggerated patience with which he said it, was getting on her nerves. "No! If you won't help him, I'll take him somewhere else."

"Mrs. Bennett, be reasonable. He's a wild animal. Even if there were something I could do for him, he'd require months of rehabilitation and then what? He wouldn't be able to go back into the wild again."

"I could take care of him," Jill said. "I take care of a lot of unwanted animals."

"Mom, stop this! Let us do our jobs and put this poor animal—"

"Rocky!"

"Rocky, then. Let us ease Rocky's pain." Rachel took Jill's arm and propelled her toward the door. "You need to go."

Jill wanted to resist, to wrench her arm free. She wanted to save Rocky, but she couldn't risk hurting Rachel. Her daughter was still so fragile. Out in the corridor, Jill pressed her forehead against the closed door to the examination room. Would it never end?

GRANT RESTED his hand on the raccoon while he waited for Rachel to return with the syringe. *Sorry, little fella, but it'll all be over soon.* He resented being thought of as heartless. He was anything but. Still, he was a realist. Animals were not people. They couldn't tell you what they wanted. He couldn't discuss treatment options or the long-term prognosis with a raccoon.

Grant wasn't sure which side he came down on in the debate about euthanasia for humans, but he hoped if he ever arrived at a hospital in as bad a condition as this poor creature, there would be no heroic act to save him.

The injection was quick and lethal. After it was over, he raised his head to look at his newest staff member.

"So that was your mom, eh?"

"Yeah, sorry about that."

"No need to apologize, I appreciate your support. It couldn't have been easy coming between us." Grant had been impressed by Rachel right from the first day she'd joined his practice. She was smart, hardworking, and driven. She knew what she wanted as only someone who'd gone through what she had ever could. And it wasn't hard to see from whom she'd gotten her good looks. Her mother was a knock-out. Too bad she was a flake. "I take it rescuing stray animals is something she does a lot?"

"It's kind of become her thing. Usually, it's dogs and cats. We had a ferret a while back. My Psych 101 prof would say she's adopted the defence mechanism of sublimation. She takes in these lost causes because she feels helpless and constantly needs to prove to herself that she can make a difference—that she can save them."

Grant had hired Rachel on the recommendation of his long-time client, Mae Pruitt. Rachel had been studying to be a veterinarian when she'd been diagnosed with ovarian cancer. Tragic, especially for someone so young. According to Mae, Rachel's mother had given up everything to nurse her daughter through the treatment.

"She did make a difference," Grant said. "You're in remission, right? You beat it. What does she have to prove?"

"It's not me she's sublimating. It's my dad."

TWO

No matter how crappy the day, you can always count on a warm reception from your furry friends.

Jill bent down and scratched Finnegan behind his ear. The one-eyed Irish Setter leaned in close, pushing her back against the door. Joss, the three-legged Corgi, snuck in between Finnegan's legs and nosed Jill's calf to get a share of the attention. Even Sacha, a left-for-dead Siamese cat, sauntered up to greet her, although he hung back waiting for Jill to finish with the dogs before he insisted on being picked up and carried into the house.

The arrogance of that man!

Tears stung her eyes and she buried her face in Sacha's velvet fur. *And my poor Rachel?* How could she work for such a monster? The cat squirmed uncomfortably, and she lowered him onto a kitchen chair.

Jill opened the refrigerator, stared at the contents, and then closed the door. She moved on to one cupboard, and then the next. She still hadn't gotten used to cooking only for herself. When there had been three of them, she'd never had any trouble coming up with menu ideas. Rachel loved pasta and casseroles and all sorts of exotic foods, while Calvin was a meat-and-potatoes man. Satisfying both had sometimes required a bit of a balancing act, but she'd always managed. She gazed around her kitchen. Why could she not think of one thing she wanted to eat, herself?

She returned to the fridge and took out the half-full bottle of Pinot Grigio she'd opened last night to soothe her nerves about starting at a new school today. No, she shouldn't be drinking every day, but today she needed its help to calm her down after her run-in with Dr. Palmer. Tomorrow would be better.

At least Rachel had tidied the kitchen before she'd left for work. That was something.

Jill took her glass and headed through the den to let the dogs out into the backyard. She sipped her wine while she waited for them to finish their business, and then brought them back in. They shook the rain off their coats, sending a shower of water droplets over her. Okay, she should have planned better and gotten a towel. Oh well, at least they were back inside with her where their breathing, burping, and farting helped break the silence of the empty house.

Rachel had brought in the newspaper and mail, too. Wow, perhaps there was hope for her daughter after all. Jill set her glass down on the coffee table. There were a couple of business-sized envelopes—bills, most likely—and a large manila-coloured one with a University of Guelph crest. Her heart clenched. It was addressed to Rachel, of course, and it had been opened.

Her hand twitched. She shouldn't. Rachel was an adult,

she deserved her privacy. But she'd left the envelope out. Maybe she wanted Jill to read it.

She took a deep breath and then a deeper gulp of wine before pulling the papers from the envelope. She stared in disbelief at the cover letter.

Rachel was planning on returning to school in January? She hadn't said anything about it, but here was a letter confirming her return to the veterinary medicine program and reinstating her scholarship.

"No!" *No, no, no.* She couldn't. She wasn't well enough to leave, yet. It had been only eighteen months since she was diagnosed. She'd undergone major surgery and then had chemotherapy. Rachel's real hair had only just started to grow back, replacing the soft fuzz that had appeared at first. It would be a while before they knew whether or not she was in full remission.

Jill leapt to her feet and spun around. How could Rachel do this to her? If she went away, who would watch over her daughter—make sure she was taken care of? What if something happened?

Stop. Breathe. Think this through.

Jill lowered herself back down onto the couch. Both Finnegan and Joss, disturbed by her movement, nosed her in concern.

"It's okay, guys. Go lie down."

It wasn't going to happen, and that was the end of it. Her daughter didn't know what she was doing. Jill would talk to her, and Rachel would just have to let the university know she wasn't ready to come back.

Jill broke down and opened a second bottle of wine while she waited for Rachel to arrive home. One more glass…

She staggered to her feet when she heard the key in the lock, and met Rachel in the hallway, waving the letter at her. "What's this?"

"I can't believe you read my personal mail!" Rachel grabbed the letter from Jill's hand.

"Don't change the subject. How can you even think of going back to school now?"

"The doctor said I was good and should resume my life."

"Not this, though. You're not ready to leave home."

"I don't think I'm the one who's not ready," Rachel said. "Besides, Guelph is only a few hours away. It's not like I'm going to the other side of the country or anything."

Rachel was right. Jill wasn't ready for her daughter to leave home. Oh dear, she shouldn't have had that last glass of wine. It was clouding her mind. Why couldn't Rachel understand? After everything... "I don't know why you would do this. After all I've done, everything I've given up—"

"You've given up? You?"

Jill backed away as Rachel barked the words at her.

"What about me? I was the one who agreed to go to Western University to do my two years of science before I could apply to vet school. Living at home to save you money, driving from St. Thomas up to the north end of London every day, not being able to live on campus—"

"We gave you a car," Jill said.

"Sure, but hardly a hardship since a new car every few years was one of Dad's perks for having twenty-plus years' seniority at the auto plant. I was the one who worked my butt off, not only to be accepted into veterinary college but to get a scholarship. And once I did, you were able to stop working."

Jill's head hurt. Why was Rachel yelling at her?

"I know you and Dad worked hard and saved your money so you could have a comfortable retirement. But it's not my fault I got cancer. And it's not my fault he died." Rachel paused and swallowed heavily. "Treating me like an invalid and taking care of all these abused and abandoned animals is not going to bring him back," she said, softening her tone. "I have to go on with my life, and you have to go on with yours. I *am* going back to school in January." She turned away, but not before Jill saw tears in her eyes. "You can't stop me."

The house reverberated as Rachel slammed the front door. Jill's stomach churned and she lowered herself onto the couch. There was a ringing in her head. Was it the wine? Maybe it was the phone.

The animals had fled when the yelling began. Poor souls. She didn't blame them after the abuse they'd suffered.

It's not my fault he died, Rachel had said, and she was right. It was Jill's.

Her head hurt. She needed the ringing to stop. Jill lurched to her feet, but the phone went silent before she could answer it. She glanced at the Caller ID. *Mae.* She probably wanted to know how Jill's first day back at work had gone. Work had been the best part of her day—the only good part.

Mae would be full of advice and well-meaning insights. Jill didn't want that now. She needed to take a couple of aspirin and drink a jug of water to flush out her system from all the wine. She was exhausted, but there was no way she'd be able to sleep before Rachel returned home.

Where did she go?

She'd call Mae back tomorrow. Tomorrow had to be better than today.

GRANT STEPPED through the doorway that led from the kennel at the back of his clinic into the rear storage area of his home. *Man, that had been one tough day.* At least he didn't have to drive home in this miserable weather.

Twice a week he remained open late—officially until nine, but it usually stretched out until well after ten. That made for an incredibly long day because he had to get up by six each morning to tend to the animals that stayed overnight. He couldn't ask his staff to come in so early. And he couldn't possibly turn away clients simply because he was running behind schedule. There was always some emergency that arose to disrupt his well-intentioned timetable. Today, it had been Rachel's mother and her raccoon.

He shook his head to dispel his irritation with himself. He'd made the right call; there was nothing that could have been done for the poor fellow—Rocky, she'd named it. And yet, ever since she'd walked out the door, Grant kept going over and over their encounter. What was it about Jill Bennett he couldn't shake? She wasn't the first bleeding heart to accuse him of being insensitive. Even Rachel, her own daughter, had thought she was being unreasonable.

"Forget it!" Grant slammed the door and kicked a pair of rubber boots out of his way.

"Well, that's a nice howdy-do." Doug grinned, a well-portioned glass of scotch in his hand. "I was just about to enjoy this, but I think maybe you need it more."

Grant took the glass from Doug. "Stealing my good stuff, are you? I thought you were more into beer." He took a generous sip, savouring the alcohol's burn as it slid down his throat. "I didn't think you'd bother coming, given the lousy weather."

Doug shrugged and turned back toward the kitchen. Grant followed him, pausing on the threshold to watch his brother grab a clean glass from the shelf and half-fill it with his good sixteen-year-old Lagavulin. Doug wasn't a drinker by nature. He'd have the occasional beer with his buddies at the volunteer fire hall on Friday night, but rarely more than one.

"You okay?" Grant asked.

Doug shrugged again, took a swig from his glass, and brushed past him to sit down in the living room. "I put the beef in the freezer. Gave you a bunch of nice cuts."

"Thanks." Grant lowered himself into the recliner beside his brother.

Doug, three years older than Grant, had taken over the family farm from their father more than a decade earlier. Once a prosperous tobacco operation, the farm had been forced to transition into cash crops as smoking became more and more of a social taboo. Even when his granddad had farmed the land in the early part of the last century, they'd raised a steer to provide an economic source of meat for the family. Despite a wife and three growing teenage boys of his own, Doug always made sure Grant got a share of the beef.

"Have you got something on your mind?" Grant asked.

"What makes you ask?"

Grant raised his empty glass to his brother's. "I don't know, you drinking maybe?"

Doug grunted and poured the rest of his scotch into Grant's glass. "Loretta wants to know if you'll come to the fireman's dinner and dance this year."

So that was the source of Doug's discomfort. Loretta was matchmaking again. "And which lovely lady are we supposed to *coincidentally* bump into this time?"

At least his brother had the decency to look embarrassed. "Mary-something-or-other," he grumbled. "I can't remember her last name. She works with Lo at the grocery. Recently divorced, I think."

"I can't believe you let your wife talk you into trying to set me up again. You'd have thought, after all these years, she'd give me up as a lost cause." Grant tossed back the rest of his scotch—*damn, that was good*—and set the glass on the table. He would be more annoyed if Doug didn't look so miserable.

"She cares, is all. She doesn't want you to be alone."

"I'm not."

"Animals don't count."

Grant chuckled. The warmth of the scotch in his belly had improved his mood. "I'm not talking about animals. I have no shortage of female companions."

Doug whirled in his chair and gaped at him.

"No, I'm not going to invite them to Sunday dinner with the family. They're not those kinds of relationships." Then, as Doug's eyes grew even wider, Grant added, "And they aren't *those* kinds of women either. I don't pay them to spend time with me. It's simply for fun—no strings, no drama."

Doug leaned back in his chair and grunted. "Doesn't sound much like companionship to me."

"I'm not the marrying kind. Been there, done that, still have the scars to prove it." Grant winced at the bitterness he heard in his voice. It had been almost eight years since he'd come home early to find Nancy in bed with his best friend. Now, if that wasn't a *cliché*, he didn't know what was. It galled him that she'd been able to convince the court that *she* was owed because of all she'd sacrificed for his career. Baloney! Ten years of marriage and she hadn't had to work a single day. Heck, half the time he'd come home and she'd want to go out for dinner rather than cook. Now she and his *bestie* were living the high life down near Windsor on the extravagant settlement her crook of a lawyer had weaselled out of him. *Good riddance!*

"So, I hear the processing plant has been bought by a foreign conglomerate. Do you think that's good or bad for you and the other cash croppers in the area?" Grant was done talking about his love life. Hopefully, Doug would take the hint and drop it, too.

"Hard to say," Doug said, looking almost as relieved by the change of subject as Grant. "The local owners were having a tough go of it—hard to compete with Mexico and its cheap labour. I don't know what the buyers are hoping to get out of the deal. I'd like to think it's just as they claim, but it smells funny."

While farming was Doug's passion, he was also a savvy businessman, who earned extra income as a tax accountant during the quiet winter season. Like most in the area, the farm couldn't generate enough income to adequately support his family, so Loretta worked as a cashier in the grocery store, and the three boys had part-time jobs in addition to school and their farm duties.

Doug stayed for another hour and they stuck to safe topics like world politics, the price of oil, and this season's expectations for the London Knights junior hockey team.

As Grant walked his brother to the door, Doug hesitated. "So, ah, what should I tell Lo?" his brother asked. "I mean, about the fireman's dinner and dance."

"For heaven's sake," Grant said, exasperated. "Okay, I'll go." It was no use. If he told Doug 'no,' Loretta would be on the phone pestering him every day until he finally gave in. He loved his sister-in-law but thank goodness he wasn't married to her. "You owe me, though. And don't blame me if things don't turn out the way Loretta wants them to."

THREE

Jill tried the door to the clinic.
Locked.
Now what?

She peered through the window. There was a light on in the back. Someone must be here. She knocked, and then pounded on the door. "Rachel! Are you there?"

"Can I— Mrs. Bennett?"

She shouldn't have been surprised to see *him* here. It was his clinic, after all. But he looked like he'd just gotten out of the shower. His dark hair was damp and his face was freshly shaved. She could smell his aftershave lotion—similar to Calvin's but with a touch more spice. No lab coat, but he was in jeans again, and a plain white T-shirt that made his eyes seem an even deeper shade of blue. They studied her warily, as if she were some sort of lunatic, come to rob the place.

"Is Rachel here?" She looked over his shoulder, scanning the waiting room for her daughter.

"No, she isn't."

Jill wilted. She hadn't thought Rachel would be. She'd just hoped…

"Come in." Dr. Palmer took her arm and led her into the clinic. "Did something happen to Rachel?"

She lowered herself onto one of the waiting room chairs. Just in time. Her knees had gone weak, and she feared her legs wouldn't support her any longer. "I don't know. She didn't come home last night."

"Mrs. Bennett—"

"Jill."

"Jill, then. Rachel's a smart girl. She wouldn't do anything stupid. She probably just got caught up with friends and forgot to call."

Even though he'd used her first name, his pacifying tone still irritated her. She glanced into his eyes and saw that, even to him, the explanation sounded feeble. "We argued and she left."

"You didn't fight about the raccoon, did you?"

Jill scowled, angry all over again about what had transpired the last time she was in this clinic.

He took a step back and held up his hands in mock defence. "I know you think I'm a jerk—"

"I think you're a monster."

Dr. Palmer's lips parted and his brows lowered. Jill immediately regretted her accusation. What type of person had she become? She used to be calm and easygoing. Now, she hardly recognized herself. She'd quarrelled with her daughter—angering Rachel to the point that she'd stormed out of the house and hadn't returned. And now she was hurtling personal insults at a virtual stranger—and Rachel's boss, no less. "I'm sorry, I shouldn't have said that. I don't know what's gotten into me. I'm usually not like this. I don't know what I'm doing or what I'm saying these days. I'm just so worried about Rachel, but that's no reason to lash out at you. Please, forgive me."

His expression softened. "I've been called worse." He held out his hand. "For a monster, I make a pretty mean cup of coffee. C'mon, I think you could use one."

She hesitated momentarily but was won over by the genuineness of his smile—and she really could benefit from the caffeine. She took his hand and allowed him to pull her to her feet, and then followed him through the clinic and into a home.

"I didn't realize you lived here, too," she said, looking around the kitchen. It was a man's kitchen: stainless steel appliances with dark countertops over heavy wooden cabinets. It would have been overwhelming except for the large eastern window that flooded the room with warm sunlight.

"Yeah, it's easier. We don't always have overnight guests in the clinic, but it happens often enough that I like to be close." He handed her a steaming mug. "Have a seat. Have you eaten anything?"

She shook her head. "Not hungry." She sat at the kitchen table, ignored the milk and sugar containers he'd placed in front of her, and sipped the hot liquid. He was right, he did make a mean cup of coffee.

He whisked two eggs and poured them into a frying pan and began chopping a red bell pepper. The sizzle and smell of the omelet made her stomach rumble, and she was secretly relieved that Grant had disregarded her statement about not being hungry, as well as the one about him being a monster.

"Did you know Rachel planned to return to vet college next semester?" Jill asked.

"Sure, she told me when she interviewed for the job." He turned toward her. "You didn't know?"

Jill's hand trembled and she set the cup down. She blinked back tears of frustration. How could Rachel tell *him* and not her own mother? "No, she didn't tell me. I found a letter from the university last night."

"You can't be surprised, though. Her treatment's over. She's beaten the cancer. Why wouldn't she want to go back?"

The innocence of Grant's question proved just how little he understood the threat ovarian cancer had posed to Rachel's life, and what it meant for her future. "It's too soon. She's just finished her treatment. We won't know her full prognosis for some time."

"But there's nothing else she can do about it now, is there? You can't expect her to sit around waiting for… whatever." His eyes had a way of penetrating Jill's outer defences, making her question herself. "Do you?"

"You, of all people, should know how stressful the veterinary medicine program is. I don't think she's ready yet. What if something happens while she's away?"

"Guelph is only a couple of hours down the highway. It's not like she's gone to the other side of the country." He turned back to the omelet and expertly flipped it onto a plate.

Rachel had said *exactly* the same thing, making Jill wonder if they had coordinated their responses in anticipation of her reaction. *Great, now you're starting to sound paranoid; seeing conspiracies everywhere.*

Grant buttered two pieces of toast and set the meal in

front of her. Jill pushed the plate away, she'd lost her appetite. He pushed it back toward her. "Look, Jill, I know you're concerned about her, but she's not a kid. I've spoken with her, she feels like she's lost almost two years of her life to this disease. She needs to move on; if only to prove to herself she's not an invalid."

Jill picked up the fork and poked at the omelet. She wasn't up for another fight. Her reserves were drained. She could only focus on one argument at a time. She realized Rachel had been through a difficult time, but so had she. She'd not only spent the last eighteen months nursing her sick daughter, she'd had to do it without the support of her husband, her rock. She hadn't even had time to mourn Calvin.

"She's got great instincts," Grant continued. "She'll be an excellent vet."

Jill shook her head. He just didn't get it.

"She's not leaving for a few months," Grant added. "I'll keep an eye on her here, and I promise to let you know if I see anything worrisome, okay?"

She looked up at him. His eyes were kind, *and* he did seem to care about Rachel's well-being. "I'd appreciate that," she said, pushing her chair back and standing. "I need to get to work. Will you have Rachel call me when she gets in?"

She was torn as she drove away. While she appreciated Grant's promise to watch out for Rachel, she couldn't help but feel resentful that her daughter felt more comfortable confiding in a man she barely knew rather than her own mother.

Grant looked up from his desk where he'd been reviewing inventory lists as Rachel hung up her coat and stashed her purse in the clinic's safe.

He'd worried, when he first hired her, that Rachel wouldn't be up to the challenge of working in a busy practice, given she'd recently finished chemotherapy. It was a gruelling procedure, very tough on the body. While she'd had some difficult days, she'd proven herself capable of managing the workload. The hardest day had been during her first week when, suddenly, her eyelashes and eye-brows had fallen out, a delayed reaction from her treatment. She seemed to have rallied from that and had recently been buoyed by the re-growth of her hair.

This morning she looked more tired than usual. Her skin was sallow, and the dark circles under her eyes were more pronounced. He felt a tug of concern and suddenly understood why Jill was so anxious. "You just missed your mom."

"She came here?" Rachel's voice cracked with indignation.

"What did you expect?" Grant rose from his desk. He'd been thinking about what he'd say to Rachel when she arrived. Jill's visit had made him uneasy. Rachel had seemed to be very conscientious and mature for her twenty-two years. Putting her mother through hell by staying out all night was not the behaviour he expected from her. "She's very worried about you."

"You don't know her. She is totally unreasonable."

"You should have told her you planned to go back to school."

"Wow, sounds like you two had quite the discussion."

Grant arched an eyebrow. "Temper tantrum?"

"I am not a child. I won't be treated like one."

"Then I suggest you stop behaving like one." Grant pointed to a chair and smiled inwardly as she stalked over to it and flopped down. She reminded him of his nephews when they were toddlers and didn't get their way. Come to think of it, he'd seen them do it as teenagers, too. Maybe rebellion was something you never grew out of. He wondered how he'd behave if his parents were still alive and called him out on some perceived misconduct or another. He'd had his share of run-ins with them when he was growing up. Would he behave differently now? He'd like to think so, but somehow…

"Look, Rachel, I am in full support of you returning to vet college in January," he said.

"Thank you. At least someone is."

"This isn't something you should have kept from your mother."

"You don't know what she's like."

"Oh, after yesterday and today, I think I do. She has focused the last few years of her life on caring for you, and you repay that by keeping a major life decision from her and punishing her for being concerned by staying out all night."

"I wasn't punishing her. I just needed some space," Rachel said, her conviction wavering.

"And a phone call saying you were all right would have been too difficult to make?"

"Okay, I'll call her and apologize."

"Thank you," Grant said. "And cut her some slack. It's not easy letting go. Your mother strikes me as an extremely passionate advocate."

"Passion is not something I'd ever associate with my mom."

"Spoken like a true daughter," Grant said. "What kid wants to think about their parents as passionate people?"

"Ewww. I wasn't thinking passion in that way. It's just my parents have always been so boring, so by-the-book."

Grant was intrigued. He hadn't meant passion in a sexual way, either, but once Rachel mentioned it, he couldn't shake the image of Jill, her auburn hair mussed from him running his fingers through it, and her whiskey eyes ablaze with desire. *Focus.* "Everyone thinks their parents are boring."

"No, mine really were. They had this plan for their future. It shaped everything they did. Mom and Dad were high school sweethearts who married right after graduation. Dad had started working for the auto plant during school breaks when he was a teenager, and he was hired on full-time and worked his way up to supervisor."

"Those were good jobs," Grant said.

Rachel nodded. "They had one child, me, because to have more would have been too expensive and disruptive to their plans. After I started school, Mom became an educational assistant so she could earn some money and still have summers off—no child care expenses, you see."

"Are you trying to tell me you had a lousy childhood?"

"Oh, goodness, no," Rachel said, quickly. "I had a great childhood. I had the perfect parents. We took camping trips and did Disney World one year. I'm just trying to get you to understand that it was all very scripted. Everyone did what was expected of them. There wasn't any…"

"Passion?"

"Exactly. I don't think I ever heard either of them raise

their voices. My parents had their entire lives mapped out. I had my scholarship to vet school. My mom had stopped working and my father was heading toward early retirement with a full pension."

"And then?"

"And then he died. My father died and I got cancer." Rachel turned her head away, but not before Grant noticed tears forming in her eyes. "I'm a lousy daughter."

"I don't think so. Jill doesn't either."

"Jill?" Rachel wiped the tears from her face and fought to hide her grin. "Now I really am curious about what you and Mom talked about."

Before he had to answer, Rachel's cell phone buzzed with a text message. From the way she jumped to grab it from her coat pocket and the pink staining her cheeks, Grant figured it was from a boy. He waited while she typed a response.

"Someone you met last night?" he asked.

"How'd you—" Rachel looked panicked. "Don't tell Mom."

"You can't keep keeping secrets from her."

"I'll tell her. Just not now."

"Then tell me." Grant had said he'd keep an eye on Rachel. At the time he'd been referring to her health, but he couldn't shake the feeling of responsibility—as if he owed it to Jill.

Rachel's smile illuminated her whole face. She looked a lot like her mother. Grant was surprised to find himself wishing he could make Jill smile—the two times he'd seen her she'd been upset. He'd bet she had a beautiful smile.

"I met up with some friends at The Ceeps, in London, last night. This guy named Austin was working there. We started talking and…I don't know…we just…clicked. He seemed to get me. No judgment, no feeling sorry for me. For the first time since this whole thing started, I felt like someone was seeing *me*, Rachel Bennett, the person, not Rachel Bennett, the cancer patient."

"So is Austin a bartender or a bouncer?"

Rachel frowned. "Speaking of judgmental."

"I'm just asking what he does," Grant said defensively, unwilling to acknowledge the gnawing protective instinct sneaking up on him.

"He's working nights as a bartender so he can be available to pick up supply teaching gigs during the day. He graduated from teachers' college last spring, but hasn't been hired on full-time anywhere, yet." She glared defiantly. "Okay?"

Grant nodded, his apprehension only slightly assuaged. "Okay."

"Okay." Rachel stood. "I'll let Connie know she can send in the first patient."

"*After* you call your mother."

JILL TOSSED a piece of carrot each to Joss and Finnegan. Sacha glared at her from a kitchen chair. "It's not my fault you don't like carrots," Jill told him and continued chopping vegetables. She'd stopped at the market after school to pick up everything she'd need to make Rachel's favourite dinner—cashew chicken stir-fry.

She resisted the pull of the Pinot Grigio chilling in the fridge. She shouldn't drink two—no, it would be three—nights in a row, and besides, she needed to have her wits about her. She'd had too much coffee already trying to compensate for her lack of sleep. Maybe later, after she and Rachel talked, she'd relax with a glass of wine—just one.

Jill was certain Grant was behind Rachel's message that she was sorry for not calling sooner and would be home for dinner. She was grateful for that.

She supposed he wasn't *so* bad. He had taken a risk by giving Rachel a job, after all. And he said he'd watch out for her. Okay, so he hadn't saved Rocky. He'd likely had to become hardened to the suffering of animals. That didn't necessarily make him a terrible person. In fact, it was a reason to sympathize with him. He probably had to make tough decisions like that all the time.

It was hard to believe he wasn't married. He was good-looking—well, pretty darn hot if she was being honest with herself and inclined to think of men that way—he was a professional with his own practice, and he made a decent cup of coffee.

The telephone rang and she checked the Caller ID. *Mae.* Shoot. She'd meant to call her back during one of her breaks today. She wiped her hands on her apron and picked up the receiver.

"Hi, Mae."

"Jill, sweetie, how ya doin'?"

Jill closed her eyes and smiled at Mae's Southern drawl—a clear indication she wasn't from Southwestern Ontario. Mae had married a long-haul truck driver and settled in the area almost forty years ago, but she'd never managed to lose her Georgia accent. Jill wondered if it wasn't a spark of defiance—that would be totally in character for the seventy-six-year-old, who'd twice battled cancer and won. They'd met at a family support group, and Mae had been her lifeline throughout Rachel's treatment.

"Hanging in, I guess. I'm getting used to the new school and routines. The kids are great, though. I have this little guy who is a holy terror—needs one-on-one attention. We can't let him in a classroom with other kids—but he's so darn cute."

"Only you, sweetie, would look at a baby crocodile and think it was cute." Mae chuckled. "And how's our girl doin'?"

Jill wanted to tell Mae everything that had happened in the last twenty-four hours, but that was too complicated a conversation to have over the telephone. Besides, she knew her friend would probably come down on Rachel's side—just like Grant had. "She's good. What's new with you?"

"Well, I was thinking we were due for a little big-girl time. Thought maybe I'd pop by with some of my fried chicken. You could whip up a salad if you insist on being healthy, too."

Jill's stomach rumbled and she could almost smell Mae's famous Southern fried chicken. But not tonight. "Sorry, Mae. I'm in the middle of cooking dinner for Rachel. We were planning on spending the evening together."

"What about later? Meet me at Ollee's for a drink?"

Jill hated putting off her friend, but she needed to make sure Rachel was her sole focus tonight. Besides, it wasn't as if Mae was on her own and lonely. She had her husband, kids, and grandkids, plus a ton of friends.

"Can I take a rain check, Mae?"

"Sure, sweetie. You just let me know when you got some time."

Jill continued to grip the receiver even after her friend hung up. Was she being selfish? Was there more to Mae's request than she'd let on?

She shook her head in annoyance. *Don't be stupid.* Mae accused her of having a knight-in-shining-armour complex, always trying to rescue somebody or something, whether they needed it or not. They hadn't seen each other for a few weeks. It was probably nothing more than a desire to get together.

The dogs roused themselves as the front door opened.

"Mom?" Rachel was home.

Jill hung up the phone. "In the kitchen."

FOUR

Jill lifted the tray of freshly baked chocolate cupcakes out of the backseat of her car and used her hip to close the door. It was a lucky coincidence that she had been able to book off the afternoon to surprise Rachel by bringing birthday treats to the clinic. The little girl Jill supported in the afternoons was participating in a class field trip and, while she would normally have gone along, this time the mother had volunteered to help.

Rachel had been asleep when Jill left for school in the morning, so she hadn't had an opportunity to wish her daughter a happy twenty-third birthday.

They had been getting along better since their talk a few weeks ago. They hadn't resolved anything—Rachel still intended to resume her studies in January and Jill was still against it—but they'd arrived at a truce whereby neither brought up the subject. It would have to be addressed eventually, but for now, they existed in a somewhat strained imitation of harmony. Rachel never failed to let Jill know if she was going out with friends after work, and she always came home at night. And Jill tried to give her daughter space, secretly hoping it would make staying home for a few additional terms more attractive.

The door to the clinic opened and a Rottweiler lunged forward, pulling a broad young man with tattoos down both arms, after it. Jill stepped back and lifted her tray above her head, hoping the dog wouldn't jump up on her. She could just imagine being knocked to the ground and having the cupcakes landing on top of her.

She hadn't looked her best the last two times she'd shown up at Rachel's work, so she'd taken extra care with her appearance this afternoon. She just wanted to look nice—for her daughter's sake. She wasn't out to impress anyone—certainly not Grant Palmer—although she had to admit she was slightly embarrassed by how she must have come across the previous times they'd met. Still, that wasn't why she'd spent three-quarters of an hour on her hair and makeup, or why she'd selected the floral tangerine-coloured dress that fit her so well. What was wrong with showing the world she was a competent, confident woman?

The man tugged on the Rottweiler's leash and led it to his vehicle. Fearing another such untimely greeting, Jill hesitated. It was always a gamble when you opened the door to a veterinary clinic. Would there be a large, excited dog eager to jump up on you or smaller dogs or cats just waiting to be tripped over?

Jill shifted the tray to balance it on one hand and gingerly pulled open the door.

"Here, let me help you." A whippet-thin older man, with heavy horn-rimmed glasses, stood up and took the tray from her. "These look lovely." He waited until Jill had closed the door and handed back the tray.

"Thanks," she said. There didn't seem to be any animals in the waiting area, at all. There didn't seem to be any other people, either. Even the Kathy Bates-look-alike receptionist wasn't at her desk. She placed the tray on the counter. "Where is everyone?"

The man shrugged and sat down. "I'm waiting for my wife. She's in with Dr. Palmer now."

Jill tried to imagine what sort of animal the man and his wife would have. Thinning gray hair wisped around his hawkish face and a brown suit jacket draped loosely from his shoulders. The matching brown trousers looked well-worn and rode up past his ankles to display a pair of dark socks tucked into bulky black orthopedic shoes. He brushed at his pants as if trying to remove an invisible crease. Probably something tiny. A Yorkie maybe.

Down the corridor, an examination room door opened and nails tapped on the linoleum as a dog limped along, its head lowered and one of his hind legs dragging.

A Beagle? She hadn't expected that.

"Yes, yes, I will let you know." The woman, a mirror image of her husband, called over her shoulder as she led her dog out into the waiting area.

"Don't wait too long, please." Kathy Bates called as she trailed the woman from the examination room.

"No, I won't." The woman followed her husband out of the clinic.

"Mrs. Bennett?" Kathy Bates—Connie, according to her name badge—circled around behind the counter, her gaze lasered-in on the tray of cupcakes. "Did you bring these for us? They look yummy."

"It's Rachel's birthday—"

"Really? She never said a thing. Your timing is perfect. We've got a bit of a break before the next patient is due. Let's take them back to the office."

Jill followed her to the back of the clinic. Rachel's initial panic at seeing her turned to mild embarrassment when Jill explained the reason for her visit and the rest of the staff insisted on singing *Happy Birthday* before diving into the treats.

"Thanks, Mom, these are great," Rachel said, polishing off her second cupcake.

Jill gave her daughter a small hug. "I'm glad." It was crazy, but she felt like she had *finally* done something right, something to make her daughter happy.

Grant's hand hovered over the tray. Jill repressed a smile. Would that be his third or fourth?

He sunk his teeth into the confection and closed his eyes as if he were experiencing Nirvana. A touch of pink icing rested at the corner of his mouth. Jill took a step toward him and then stopped herself. What was she thinking?

Grant's eyes flew open and his brows arched quizzically as he grinned at her. He'd caught her. "Do I have icing all over my face?" He ran his fingers around his mouth but managed to miss the spot.

"Just a bit," Jill moved to him. "Right there." Using her thumb, she wiped it away. He stared at her, eye-to-eye, for several long seconds. The humour disappeared from his face and she felt a rush of crimson stain her cheeks as she realized how intimate her action had been.

She glanced at Connie and the technician, who'd been introduced as Sami, but neither seemed to notice her embarrassment. She chanced a quick peek at Rachel, but she, too, seemed unaware of Jill's gaff. *Whew!* "I should let you all get back to work." Desperate to cover her awkwardness, she spoke too loudly. She took a deep breath and turned to her daughter. "How about a late birthday supper? I can make your favourite."

"Sorry, Mom. I've got plans to meet up with some friends to celebrate tonight. Can we do something on the weekend?"

"Sure," Jill said, trying to hide her disappointment.

The fine hairs on the back of her neck prickled as she muttered a quick goodbye. Grant didn't move. He merely regarded her, a puzzled expression on his face.

She couldn't get out of the clinic fast enough.

GRANT WATCHED Jill disappear through the waiting room and turned to Rachel. "So, you still haven't told her about Austin, eh?"

At least she had the decency to look chagrined. "I will when the time is right."

He shook his head. *Let it go*, he told himself as he returned to his office. She wasn't his child. He wasn't responsible for her actions, and he could only do so much to encourage her to be honest with her mother. At least they seemed to be getting along better.

Jill's visit and her cupcakes had come at the right time. They were a perfect antidote for the emotional meeting he'd just had with his last patient. He hated being the bearer of bad news, but he couldn't sugar-coat the truth. His clients expected honesty from him, and although he'd tried to be as gentle as he could with Mrs. Simmons, there was no way to put a positive spin on Sherlock's situation. The four-year-old Beagle was in great pain from a herniated disc.

The owners had already spent a considerable sum of money on a complete neurological work-up to confirm the intervertebral disc disease diagnosis. The treatment called for an even more costly surgery. However, given how far the disease had already progressed and the amount of rehabilitation that would be required afterwards, Grant had recommended they euthanize the dog. The Simmons had neither the money nor the physical stamina to ensure a successful outcome.

He'd given Mrs. Simmons some heavy-duty painkillers for Sherlock but urged her to make her decision quickly. There was no sense in prolonging the dog's suffering.

He leaned back in his chair and closed his eyes, the taste of chocolate still in his mouth. And the icing…

Those were freaking-fantastic cupcakes. He licked his lips, remembering her gentle touch on his mouth. Jill wasn't bad, either. Yessiree, the woman cleaned up nicely. His body stirred as he thought about how her dress had clung to her hips, stopping just above her knees to showcase her fantastically long, lean calves. And the shape of her ass as it swayed out the door…

He shivered in anticipation…but of what he didn't know. His senses heightened and he was on edge. This was becoming an annoyingly frequent sensation whenever Grant thought about Jill Bennett. He tried not to, but it was tough. Every time he saw the daughter he was reminded of her mother. It was probably a good thing Rachel wasn't going to be around much longer.

"Mom stop!"

Grant snapped out of his contemplation of Jill's ass and hurried to the door to see the woman, herself, marching toward him, poor stoned Sherlock in her arms, and a frantic Rachel behind her. *What now!*

Jill was panting from the exertion of carrying the slightly obese Beagle.

"What are you doing with him?" Grant asked.

"His poor owners have been sitting in their car all this time, desperately trying to figure out what to do. How can you be so cruel?"

"I'm being realistic," Grant said.

"Mom, you need to stop this." Rachel reached out to take the dog.

"You are refusing to treat a sick animal?" Jill ignored her daughter and focused the full brunt of her fury on Grant.

"It's not that simple," he said. He could see she was on the verge of tears. This was worse than the raccoon incident. He already felt bad about Sherlock. He didn't need Jill's condemnation, too. "The treatment is long and expensive. Sherlock is already partially paralyzed by the disease. There is no guarantee he'd recover. I can't, in good conscience, recommend surgery when the odds of success are low *and* I know the Simmonses are on a fixed income."

"You don't have to charge them for it."

"What?"

"You heard me. You could do it for free, or at a reduced rate, out of the goodness of your heart. Oh, I forgot. You don't have one."

That stung. He closed his eyes and tried to block out

the sound of Rachel and Jill arguing while he attempted to form a rational rebuttal. He couldn't take on every charity case that presented itself; there were far too many, some more compelling, and most with a greater chance of success than this one. But the look on Jill's face... Darn it. He hated tears.

No, he couldn't—wouldn't—do it. He pushed away all sentiment and assumed his most authoritative manner and tone. "While Sherlock is a poor candidate for surgery, that is only part of it. Afterwards, he'd require an extensive period of complete rest for the healing to occur. He'd have to be in a well-padded area and turned every few hours to prevent bedsores. He'd require assistance with urination, defecation, eating, and drinking."

"That's all doable." Jill shifted the dog to a more comfortable position in her arms.

"Physical therapy, acupuncture, and massage would be required," he continued as if she hadn't interrupted him.

"Again, not a problem."

"And even with all that, about fifty percent of the time, symptoms reoccur." Grant reached for the dog. Jill reluctantly passed him over. When he had him securely in his arms, Grant scratched him behind his ears. Sherlock's eyes were glassy and his breathing laboured.

Grant knew this wasn't really about Sherlock. Jill was transferring her fears for Rachel into her concern for the dog. He tried again. "It would be hard on a human being to go through all that—and they would know what was going on. This poor fellow would have months of pain to look forward to and no awareness that there'd be an end in sight."

"But the treatment *could* work," Jill insisted.

Grant sighed. "Yes, of course. But you've seen Mr. and Mrs. Simmons. They're well into their eighties. Money aside, do you think they have the physical stamina to handle everything that is required for Sherlock's recovery? And then, after it's all done, the best way to avoid recurrence is to ensure the dog stays a healthy weight by getting a lot of exercise."

"I could do it," Jill said.

Grant raked his fingers through his hair and opened his mouth to continue the argument, but Jill interrupted.

"I could. I could do it all."

He should have expected that. Grant was torn between frustration with her unwillingness to see reason and admiration for her determination to fight for what she believed in. He knew Rachel's cancer had been caught early, but he wouldn't doubt that a good part of her recovery was due to Jill's refusal to accept any other outcome.

He gave Sherlock one last rub behind his ears and put him back into Jill's arms. "I'll have Connie prepare an estimate for you."

FIVE

Jill lowered her gaze, afraid she would see the I-told-you-so look on Grant's face. At least the late autumn rain hid her tears. But her red eyes? That was another story.

She hated coming to him, but she'd had no choice. It was Sunday and her own, more sympathetic, vet was closed. She'd hoped to be able to wait until Monday morning, but Sherlock would no longer swallow his pain medication and she couldn't bear to see him suffer any longer.

Since taking the Beagle home with her earlier in the week, Jill had barely gotten any sleep. Sherlock howled all the time, disturbing the other animals. Rachel had purchased earplugs so she could sleep through the night. And during the day, Jill's concern for the dog affected her concentration at work so much that she raced home to check on him during her lunch hour. She was exhausted and desperate.

Grant had warned her, but Jill was still shocked when

Connie presented her with the estimate for surgery. "It's one of the most expensive surgeries there is," Connie had said.

She had gotten a second quote from Dr. Vanderhorst, but she'd wanted to charge even more.

Jill wished the cost didn't matter, but it did. Calvin's premature death had robbed her of a significant portion of the pension they'd been counting on, and while much of Rachel's treatment was covered by government health care, many of the additional expenses had slowly drained her bank account. She'd told everyone she was returning to work because she needed something to occupy her days, but the truth was she needed the money more.

"Please help him," Jill pleaded.

Grant whisked past her, bare-footed, to retrieve Sherlock from her car. Jill followed him into his home, down the hallway toward where the house and clinic connected. "Wait here," he said, nodding toward the kitchen as they passed it. "There's coffee."

Jill ignored it, trailing behind. She didn't want to let Sherlock out of her sight.

Grant laid the dog carefully onto an examination table. He expelled a gasp of exasperation when Jill stepped in the doorway. "I'm not sneaking him off to euthanize him," he snapped.

A guilty heat washed through her. That was precisely what she was afraid he'd do.

Grant bent over Sherlock, giving him a cursory examination. "Despite what you think, I don't play God with my patients." He carried the dog to a crate, not looking at her as he set up an intravenous drip. "I spent years at school so I could provide the best possible *advice*, but it's up to you to decide whether you accept it or not."

He did care. Jill could see it in his gentle movements and the way he spoke softly, soothingly to the dog while he waited for whatever he had given him to work its magic.

For the first time in her life, she felt completely helpless. When Calvin died, even in her numb emotional state, she'd known what to do: arrange his funeral, register his death, send change of contact information to all the bill collectors... When Rachel was diagnosed only weeks later, she'd immersed herself in the cancer world, overseeing every aspect of her daughter's treatment. Even Finnegan, Joss, and Sacha, as vulnerable as they were when she'd adopted them, had never challenged her as did this situation with Sherlock.

Jill wandered back to the kitchen and sat down at the table. She was too tired even to pour herself a cup of coffee.

Eventually, Grant returned. "He's comfortable. I've given him something to control the pain and help reduce inflammation." He poured two cups of coffee and handed her one, before sitting down across from her.

She could feel his gaze on her, and she slowly raised her head to meet it. She'd expected to see pity or, maybe, disgust. She'd messed up. Instead, she saw compassion and concern, and she felt a deep thud in her chest.

"You hold on too tightly," he said.

She looked away. "You're wrong. I didn't hold on tightly enough. I took my life for granted and I lost everything.

"You can't blame yourself for Rachel getting cancer."

"Can't I?" She turned back to him. "Two years ago, I had everything. I was actually *happy* that Rachel was away at school. I felt like I had completed that phase of my life; my role as a mother of a child was over. Job well done. Yay me." She paused to breathe.

If she had known that was to be their last Christmas together as a family, if she had known when she'd left the house that evening, it was going to be the last time she'd see her husband alive, if she had known her life was going to change so dramatically in a few short weeks, she would have taken more care to savour every moment of the journey that had brought her to that point.

Grant cocked his head, his expression serious. "This is about more than Rachel, isn't it?"

"I should have saved him. Calvin. My husband."

"What could you have done?"

They'd had a wonderful Christmas. Rachel had returned to Guelph to begin her second semester of vet studies and, while Jill and Calvin loved having their daughter home, they were also enjoying their new childless status. Ordering Chinese take-out in the middle of the week had felt so decadent that Jill thought she'd go for broke and stopped at the liquor store to pick up a bottle of wine, too. At that time, wine was a rare celebratory drink.

If only she had come straight home.

The paramedics said there was nothing she could have done. Calvin had suffered a massive heart attack and had probably been dead before he hit the floor. But wasn't that what they always said to make the family feel better?

"I should have been there," she said.

Jill's life was now divided in two: the period before

Calvin's death and her daughter's cancer diagnosis, and the period following. The first was a blur because she hadn't taken the time to appreciate what she'd had. She'd be damned if she'd allow that to happen to the second.

"Are you worried there's a genetic component to Rachel's cancer?" Grant asked.

"Calvin died of a heart attack which had nothing to do with Rachel. And it doesn't matter, anyway. She'll never have children."

"I'm sorry."

"She *was* tested for the BRCA mutation, though. There was a concern that if she had it, she could develop breast cancer, too."

"Oh, Jill, I'm so sorry. I don't know what to say."

No one ever knew what to say when they found out her daughter, at age twenty-one, had been diagnosed with ovarian cancer. At least Grant had the respect to admit it. Not everyone did and she'd had more than her fair share of people's strange and awkward reactions.

"She was negative, thank goodness," Jill said. "The doctors said her cancer was a random fluke of nature. We caught it early—stage 1C—which I'm told is lucky, as if anything about this can be considered *lucky*. They removed her reproductive organs to make sure they got it all. She would have had both breasts removed, too, if the BRCA test had been positive."

She was talking too much. Grant probably didn't want to hear any of this. She was so tired her usual social filters weren't working. She glanced up at him. He seemed interested, though, and didn't appear to be the least bit squeamish about the subject.

"What's next for her? She seems strong. Healthy," he said.

"We keep monitoring her, hoping, praying it won't come back. The doctors say her prognosis is good, that there's no reason to believe they didn't get it all, and that her likelihood of developing another form of cancer is no more or less than anyone else."

"And what about you?"

"There's no reason to suppose I will get it."

"That's not what I meant. What are you going to do now that Rachel is set to go on with her life?"

Jill shrugged. She didn't know how to answer the question. She hadn't allowed herself to think beyond the next day for so long now, she'd forgotten how to plan a future. Perhaps that was for the best. Living for the future had robbed her of it; better to hang on to the present. Keep to the familiar, keep to what was safe.

"What about you, Dr. Palmer?" she said to change the subject. "Why is there no Mrs. Palmer?" Her face flamed with the intimacy of the question. Crappy lack of filters. "Forget that. It's none of my business."

Grant laughed and she felt herself go even redder. "It's okay. There *was* a Mrs. Palmer, once, I'm sorry to say. But we ended up being just another divorce statistic."

"I'm sorry," Jill said. The bitterness in his tone told her that he hadn't been the one to initiate the break-up, and she felt compassion for his pain. But why should that make her feel closer to him? Was he more appealing knowing that he, too, had been robbed of his life partner? That he believed marriage was supposed to be forever?

Her fatigue was making her overly sentimental. Maybe his wife left him because he was a jerk.

"It's okay. We're both much happier now," he said.

Was that sarcasm?

"It's almost lunch time. Are you hungry?" he asked.

Jill's stomach rumbled at the mention of food. She hadn't been eating properly and had skipped breakfast this morning.

"I'll take that as a 'yes,'" Grant said, winking at her. "I'm going to go check on Sherlock. Why don't you look in the freezer? I think there are a couple of steaks we can barbecue, and I've got stuff to make a salad in the fridge."

Jill had almost finished preparing the salad when Grant returned to announce that Sherlock was resting well. She was grateful he wasn't pushing her to decide the dog's fate just yet.

Grant picked up the large steak Jill had set on the counter and began removing the brown wrapper. "Ah, K, a very good year."

Jill had noticed different letters written on the various packages in the freezer. "What does K mean?"

"K is for Kedar"

"And what is Kedar?"

His grin lit up his face and he wagged his eyebrows at her. "Kedar was a son of Abraham. Don't you know your Bible?"

"So?" Jill knew he was teasing her, but he looked so boyishly pleased with himself she couldn't muster the energy to be annoyed.

"Kedar is also the name of the steer from which this steak came," he said.

"You label your beef with the name of the cow it came from?"

"Steer," he corrected. "And of course, how else do you know the age of the beef?"

"I don't know. You could put a date on it."

"Now where would the fun be in that?" Grant said. "I can tell precisely how old the meat is: K for Kedar is this year—Doug just brought it to me a few weeks ago. J, for Jonah—the one who survived three days in the belly of a whale, remember?—is from last year. And if you come across an I—that's Isaiah—you'd better feed him to the dogs because he's two years old and probably has freezer burn."

Jill's shoulders shook, belying an attempt to suppress her laughter. Finally, she couldn't hold it in any longer and she doubled over, tears forming in her eyes. "That has got to be the strangest system I've ever heard of," she said when she could finally speak. "It's kind of barbaric, don't you think? Cannibalistic, even."

"They're cattle, Jill."

"But it's like you *know* them."

Grant shook his head in mock disgust, but his eyes shone with humour. "It's not like we have a deep personal relationship or anything."

Jill looked at the package in his hand and grimaced.

"You're not a vegetarian, are you?"

She shook her head. Jill loved a grilled steak as much as anyone. "It's just that I never thought about where meat comes from before. I mean before it gets to the store."

"Most city people don't, or at least they don't want to. Remember the old slogan: If you ate today, thank a farmer?"

"All right," Jill giggled. "Let's see if Kedar was a good year."

Grant waved goodbye to Sami, locked the clinic door, and returned to his own home. Jill was still sound asleep on the couch where he'd left her several hours earlier.

Sami hadn't asked any questions when he'd called to ask her to come in and help with an emergency surgery. He didn't know why he did it. And he sure as hell wasn't convinced it had been the right thing to do.

But when he saw Jill laugh—he'd done that, made her happy—it had felt amazingly good.

He was such an idiot. There was a huge gulf between making a woman chuckle at a ridiculous story and undertaking a risky and expensive surgery on an animal with less than even odds of recovering, just to see her smile.

Jill stirred and sat up. "Is something wrong? Is it Sherlock?"

"No, he's fine," Grant said, sitting down beside her. "I'm going to keep him for a while."

"It's not fair to him, is it?" she whispered hoarsely. She lowered her head to her hands. Her voice was muffled and he had to strain to hear her. "I'm so sorry. You were right. I was being selfish. I was the one playing God, not you. You were just being realistic." Her sobbing intensified. "I can't bear to see him in constant pain and I can't afford the surgery. Even if I could, I'm not sure how I'd manage everything you said needs to be done afterwards." She raised her head, her expression raw agony. "I just wanted to save him, you know?"

Grant took her hand and squeezed it gently. This woman constantly amazed him with the depth of her passion and her strength of will. He couldn't imagine how much it had cost her to admit defeat.

"I believe I was successful at relieving the pressure on his spinal cord," he said. "I'll keep him here at the clinic during his recovery period, and we can figure out how to handle the rehabilitation once we have a better idea of what he needs."

He watched her confused expression slowly transform to understanding.

"You did the surgery?" She gaped at him.

He nodded. There it was, the smile, the joy he wanted to see—the reason he'd done it. She squealed with glee and wrapped her arms around his neck, pulling him toward her.

Her lips were soft and he held his breath, expecting her to back away after a quick 'thank you' peck. Instead, she paused, her mouth only a kiss away. She expelled a soft, warm breath that fanned his lips. It was likely only a fraction of a second, but time seemed suspended. Was she waiting for him?

He reached for her. His fingers threaded through her messy curls and he held her head as he leaned in to claim her mouth. She shifted closer, and he groaned as her hip brushed across his lap.

He deepened the kiss, teasing open her lips so his tongue could enter her mouth. Man, she tasted good.

She felt good, too. One hand continued to play in her hair while he lowered the other along the contour of her cheek, down her neck, along her collarbone, to her shoulder—

Jill gasped and pulled away. "I'm so sorry. I don't know what got into me."

Grant's body hummed with tension and he ached with the realization that relief wasn't coming. He took a deep breath. What had he been thinking? First the damned dog and now this?

She looked stricken and he pushed aside his physical discomfort. She wasn't responsible for this. "It's okay," he said. "It's a nice way to be thanked—better from you than Mrs. Simmons." He forced a sheepish grin and was rewarded by a tentative smile from Jill.

"Can I see Sherlock?"

"Sure." Grant allowed her to get up first and head to the door. While her back was to him, he rose and quickly adjusted his pants to hide the obvious tenting. It didn't help that he couldn't stop staring at her ass as she led the way into the clinic.

This has got to stop.

He had nothing to offer her but sex—and heaven knows he wanted to make love to her—but she wasn't that kind of woman. She was vulnerable. The mother of one of his employees. A widow, for heaven's sake.

She probably hadn't slept with anyone since her husband died. And before then? Who knows what went on in their marriage? Rachel had called her family boring, but his every encounter with Jill had revealed a woman full of passion. Definitely not boring.

The humming throughout his body was back.

She's not the type of woman you date, Palmer.

And yet, to his horror, he heard himself ask her to go with him to the firemen's dinner and dance the following weekend.

Crap!

SIX

"Is it my imagination or am I the most hated woman in the room?"

"I wouldn't say hated." Grant's sister-in-law, Loretta, giggled. "Certainly, speculated about."

From the moment she and Grant arrived at the firemen's dinner and dance, Jill had felt piercing scrutiny from the community—especially from the women. Everyone was very polite when Grant introduced her, but she could feel hostility radiating from the unattached women in the room and unabashed curiosity from the men.

Grant seemed oblivious to the stares and glares being thrown their way. He'd stayed by her side during the pulled-pork dinner, and had asked her to dance as soon as the music started.

She watched him move on the dance floor with Mary-something, a fortyish bleached-blonde, who looked like the stereotyped desperate divorcee on the prowl—tight leopard-patterned leggings, low-cut top displaying ample cleavage, and lots of shiny jewellery competing for attention with her overly made-up face. She'd been circling Grant all evening and, finally, Jill had urged him to accept her request to dance, if only to get a little breathing room.

Jill had seen the look of astonishment that had passed between Loretta and her husband, Doug, when they'd arrived for the dinner. She wasn't sure if they were more surprised that Grant had actually shown up, or that he'd brought a date. He'd warned Jill about small-town gossip and explained that it was one of the reasons he'd moved to St. Thomas, although, truth-be-told, St. Thomas was hardly a thriving metropolis. Even there, he was viewed as one of the most eligible bachelors, according to Mae. If he were looking for anonymity, he'd have been better off going to Toronto. However, with his good looks and charismatic personality, she doubted even Canada's largest city would be big enough for him to hide in.

Jill had liked Loretta immediately. She was a strong, determined woman, who spoke her mind, but in the most loving and well-intentioned way. It was obvious she was the one running her family, and equally obvious that her husband and three sons doted on her. She possessed a natural beauty with big green eyes and a wide friendly smile. There was nothing pretentious about Loretta Palmer. She wore little makeup, didn't try to hide her grey-streaked brown hair with dye, and dressed modestly in a short-sleeved, floral-printed dress that covered her chest and fell below her knees. Even her low-heeled Mary Janes were practical for an evening of dancing.

By contrast, Jill had chosen a short jade green form-flattering dress and less-than-comfortable high-heels, which she'd kicked off after the first dance. She was wearing more makeup than usual due to Rachel's insistence. She had been nervous about how her daughter would react when she learned of her date with Grant, but Rachel had been enthusiastic, insisting on helping with her makeup and hair. Jill raised a hand to her unruly curls, which had shaken loose of the clasp during dancing. *Oh well, it was nice while it lasted.*

The song ended. Grant was leading a reluctant Mary-something off the dance floor when the music changed into a slow romantic tune. Another woman—Jill couldn't remember her name—made a beeline toward the pair and tried to drag Grant back onto the floor. Mary-something was having none of this, taking Grant's other arm and insisting he dance with her.

"This is the most entertainment I've had in a long time." Loretta chortled. "Usually, these things are so deadly dull—same people, same conversation. But this is better than an episode of *The Bachelor*!"

Jill joined her laughter. She was enjoying the show, too. Poor Grant looked like he was about to be pulled into two pieces. Suddenly, he shook his arms free, sending Mary-something and the other woman spinning away, and stomped toward Jill. He held out his hand. "Dance." More of a statement than a request.

She followed him onto the dance floor. As he pulled her close, she remembered that, in her bare feet, they were about the same height. Strange. He always felt bigger than her, even when she was in heels. She wrapped her arms around his neck, and he rested his cheek against hers. He was warm and solid and smelled of sweat and aftershave—a heady, musky scent that stirred something deep inside of her. Something she hadn't felt for a very long time. It both frightened and exhilarated her. She shivered and he pulled her closer.

They didn't speak. Jill closed her eyes and trusted Grant to lead. She felt safe and protected in his arms. Another slow song followed the first. His cheek was smooth, and she knew if they turned their heads the slightest bit, their lips would meet. She flushed. She couldn't believe she'd kissed him the other day. It was so unlike her. But the way he'd responded...the way she'd responded...

She felt a damp heat between her breasts, and lower, in her abdomen.

She'd never been with any man other than her husband and had only rarely fantasized about making love with someone else.

Whoa! Was that what she was thinking of doing with Grant? That she wanted to end the night in his bed?

Fiery moisture pooled between her thighs.

The song ended and the drum-beat intro signalled a switch to a faster-paced dance number. As they stepped apart, Jill noticed Mary-something galloping toward them.

"Let's get out of here," Grant whispered, threading his fingers through hers and gently pulling her off the dance floor.

They said a quick goodbye to Loretta and Doug, and to his three nephews who were sitting outside with the other teenagers who were too cool to dance alongside their parents.

"Let's never do that again," Grant said, as he slid into the driver's seat of his SUV.

Jill exploded into laughter, and after two seconds,

Grant joined her. "You should have warned me that I was taking my life in my hands by coming here," she said when they were finally able to contain themselves. "Next time I'll wear a Kevlar vest to protect me from the daggers being thrown my way."

Grant's gaze raked over her. "Next time, I'd like to see you in full body armour."

He made it sound sexy, and Jill felt a blush creep into her cheeks.

He chuckled at her reaction, started the engine, and pulled onto the highway.

Jill glanced at the dashboard clock as they passed the St. Thomas welcome sign. It was only ten-thirty. They'd be at her house in a couple of minutes and the evening would be over.

"Would it be okay if I stopped in to see Sherlock before you take me home?" she asked. She'd visited Sherlock every day since his surgery, including earlier today. She hadn't always seen Grant at the clinic because he was often with patients, but that wasn't why she'd been going —or so she told herself.

"Sure," he said and drove past the turn-off for her street.

Grant had told Jill he was both pleased and surprised by the dog's recovery. He expected the Beagle would be allowed more movement this week, and some sort of physiotherapy would begin shortly after.

Sherlock greeted her with a soft tap of his tail against his crate. She gently rubbed the dog's forehead, wondering what the heck she'd been thinking by inviting herself back to Grant's home. It had been exciting to be on the arm of the most eligible bachelor at the dance, and she'd thoroughly enjoyed the evening, but the dance was over.

She turned off the light in the recovery room and walked back to the kitchen where Grant waited for her.

"I poured you a glass of wine," Grant said when he saw her. "Pinot Grigio, right? Rachel said it was your favourite."

"Thanks." She accepted the glass, her hand shaking slightly. He'd asked Rachel about her favourite wine? He was either incredibly thoughtful or... She took a sip, savouring the tangy citrus flavour in her mouth and the cool rush as it flowed down her throat. They'd only served beer and cheap liquor at the dance.

She was trembling. She didn't know what to expect. She didn't even know what she wanted to happen.

She watched Grant over the rim of her glass. He leaned back comfortably against the counter and rolled the wine around his glass, eyeing it suspiciously.

"Not a wine drinker?" she asked.

"Not usually. This isn't bad, though. I could grow to like it. A lot."

The way he said "a lot" made her skin tingle and the look he was giving her seemed to indicate he was talking about much more than the wine. But it had been so long since she'd done anything like this...well, she'd never had. She'd been a teenager when she and Calvin began dating.

Was Grant waiting for her to say something? Make the first move? Women did that these days, she'd heard.

Goodness, he was handsome with his tousled dark hair, striking blue eyes, and roguish grin—not to mention great physique. In a dark purple pin-striped dress shirt and tight black denim jeans, it was no wonder the women at the dance were in a frenzy over him. And he was here with her. Why?

"Look—" she began, but he interrupted her, which was just as well since she hadn't been at all sure what she'd intended to say.

"Jill." He put his glass on the counter and stepped toward her. He took her wine and set it on the table. With one hand, he gently cupped her face and she found herself lost in his eyes.

"I—" She tried again to speak.

"Shhh," he whispered, slowly leaning in.

As soon as his lips touched hers, she melted into him and wrapped her arms around his neck. His free arm encircled her hips, pulling her in closer. She tasted the Pinot on his lips and moaned as he slipped his tongue into her mouth.

She wriggled in closer, excited by the dual sensation of his large warm hand cupping her bottom while the bulge in his jeans strained at the juncture between her thighs.

His fingertips brushed over her cheek before threading into the thick curls that had fallen around her face. He broke away from her mouth to trail small kisses down her cheek and along her chin. She arched backward, giving him easier access to her neck. Grant murmured something she couldn't quite make out. It sounded like "beautiful," but she couldn't be sure.

His hands slid to the zipper at the back of her dress. She felt a tug and then a rush of cool air on bare skin as the fabric slipped open.

For a quick moment, Jill congratulated herself on her purchase of the lacy violet bra and panty set, and then she chastised herself. That made her sound scheming. It wasn't as if she bought it expecting this to happen.

Or had she? She'd wanted to look nice and feel…sexy.

All rational thought quickly disappeared when Grant's hand covered one lacy breast and he lowered his mouth to suckle at the other through the fabric.

His free hand worked its way through the zipper opening to caress her bottom. Her hips rolled in rhythm and his erection grew, digging deeper between her legs.

She was frantic to feel him, to touch his skin, to taste him. Her hands shook as she drew his shirt free from his jeans. She fumbled with the buttons until she was able to run her hands along his naked shoulders, and down the plane of his back, feeling the strength of him.

She felt flushed and dizzy. Her nipples were aflame as Grant nuzzled one and toyed with the other. She wanted him to touch her, skin-to-skin. Jill reached behind and unclipped her bra. She heard him gasp as it fell away.

So much better, but not nearly enough. Sweet hot desire spiralled downward. She unbuckled his belt and then undid his jeans before pushing them down over his hips where they fell heavily to the floor. She cupped his bottom through his boxer briefs and then reached around the front and under the waistband—

Grant seized her wrist. "Are you sure?" His voice was hoarse and his breathing ragged. "Because I don't want you to do anything you don't want to. We can stop."

"I don't want to stop." Jill's voice was but a breathless whisper. "I'm sure."

"Thank God." He whisked her up into his arms and carried her into his bedroom.

SEVEN

"Oh my gosh! Is that really the time?"

Jill lurched up, instinctively clutching the sheet to keep herself covered. The glowing red numbers on the digital clock read 3:45. She must have dozed off.

Grant lay beside her, his head propped on one arm and looking wide awake. He grinned and rolled to push her back down onto the bed. "The night's still young."

Jill was torn. A big part of her wanted to stay with him, but how would it look? What would Rachel say if she didn't come home? "No, no, no, I can't spend the night."

Grant ignored her protest as he kissed his way along her collarbone, moving lower toward her breasts, pulling the sheet down as he descended. It felt so wonderful. "Please, Grant. Stop."

He raised his head, his eyes questioning. "Are you sure?" His voice was teasing, suggestive.

No, she wasn't sure. She wanted more than anything to stay with him and make love again and again. But the clock now said 3:47. Jill took a deep breath to steady herself. She had to get home. "I'm sorry," she said. The words sounded inadequate to her, but she couldn't think of what else she could say.

He sighed, sat up, and swung his legs over the side of the bed. "Okay, give me a minute. I'll drive you."

Jill started to wrap the sheet around herself so she could go retrieve her clothes, and then dropped it. She'd just spent the last few hours allowing this man to explore every inch of her body, covering it up now seemed ludicrous.

She could feel Grant's gaze on her as she dressed. He didn't move until she pulled the dress up over her shoulders. Then he came behind her and slowly raised the zipper while nuzzling the sensitive hollow beneath her ear. "Last chance," he murmured.

She moaned, sorely tempted. Would a few more hours be that bad? "Sorry." There was that lame expression again. "I don't want Rachel to worry," she added, feeling the need to offer more of an explanation. Surely, he'd understand. He'd seen how frantic she'd been when Rachel hadn't come home that night.

She leaned back against Grant, pushing away all thought to savour a last few moments of bliss.

He wrapped one arm around her abdomen and hugged her close. "Rachel's probably not even home." His voice was low and hoarse, and it took her a few seconds to comprehend what he'd said.

She swung around to face him. "What are you talking about? Why wouldn't she be home?"

Obviously startled, Grant abruptly stepped away. He picked up his jeans, keeping his back to her as he pulled them on.

"Grant, look at me! What did you mean when you said 'Rachel's probably not even home'?"

"What I should have said is she's not likely to be worried about you because she knows you're with me." Grant turned to face her.

"But that's *not* what you said." She wished he'd put a shirt on. His bare chest was too distracting and she had the feeling she needed all her wits about her now.

"No," he said carefully. He seemed to be considering his options, which heightened her concern.

What was he keeping from her? Was Rachel sick again? Was she at the hospital? She'd been overly helpful in getting Jill ready for tonight, almost pushing her out the door. Jill recalled Rachel's parting words: *Don't hurry home.* "Is she okay? Is it the cancer? Has it come back?"

"Oh, God, no," Grant said quickly. "No, I'd never let her keep something like that from you. Rachel is fine."

"What would you let her keep from me, then?" Jill's initial sense of dread was turning into anger. It was obvious he was hiding something. She thought they were a team where her daughter was concerned. He said he'd help keep an eye on her—keep her safe.

"It's not a big deal." Grant ran his hands through his hair. He looked guilty and defensive. "Let me make you a coffee before you go."

"I'm very wide awake right now. Stop stalling."

"I'm not stalling. I think this is something Rachel should tell you, herself." He took a step toward her, but her glare stopped him. "It's not a bad thing."

She waited. She'd never seen Grant look uncertain before.

"Okay, fine," he said, exasperated. "She met this guy. I think it's getting pretty serious."

A guy? "When did she meet him?" Jill was impressed that she managed to keep her voice calm despite her desire to scream at him. If Grant saw her losing it, he'd adopt his vet-delivering-bad-news persona and she'd lose her advantage over him.

"She met him that night when she didn't come home—"

"You mean she slept with him the first night she met him?" Jill was appalled. She thought Rachel was smarter than that.

"No. They spent the night talking. She was upset and said he helped her work through things. She said it was refreshing to be with someone who didn't treat her like a cancer patient."

Jill had no idea her daughter felt she was treated differently because of her illness. "Does this *guy* have a name?"

"His name is Austin."

"Have you met *Austin*? What does he do? How old is he?"

"He's been around a couple of times. He graduated from teachers' college last spring. I think you're making too much of this. He seems like a nice guy. He makes her happy."

How could Grant possibly know what made Rachel happy? She'd only been working with him for a few months. Jill had known her daughter her whole life. She'd been there when Rachel had giggled at the wonder of blowing bubbles for the first time, seen her smile from ear-to-ear after she'd successfully ridden her bicycle to the end of the street and back, and snuggled with her as they'd read all four books of the *Twilight* series and then watched each of the five movies—go Team Edward. Jill had helped her dress for her first date and dried her tears after her first heartbreak. She'd been to every school concert, ceremony, and commencement. They'd stood together as Calvin was laid to rest and they'd fought together to beat this horrible disease called ovarian cancer. How dare Grant presume to know her daughter better than she did?

Rachel was still in denial about so much of her future. Did Grant know that? She'd bet her last dollar that Austin didn't.

"Look, she's an adult," Grant said. "You can't keep protecting her. You need to let her experience life. Live it."

"And yet, this *adult* feels the need to hide from her mother that she has a boyfriend?"

"She's worried about your reaction. She just wants to spend some time with the guy—get to know him without the pressure of..." He let the sentence hang unfinished.

"Without the pressure of what?" Jill knew what he'd been going to say: without the pressure of a crazy cancer-obsessed mother.

"You *do* tend to be a little over-protective," Grant said, lightly. When she didn't respond to his attempt to break the tension, he became serious again. "Jill, it's not a bad thing to worry about your daughter—especially after what you've both been through. She just needs a little space right now."

"First, you say you know what makes her happy, and now you presume to know what *my* daughter needs? How could you? You don't know what she's been through—

what we've both been through." Heat flared in her face. So, what if he thought she was a cancer-obsessed mother? "Do you know what it's like to look at your child—your baby—lying in a hospital bed and not know if she's going to live or die? To watch her become weaker and weaker from the treatment that's supposed to help her? To pretend to be strong for her while inside you're terrified you're going to outlive your child?"

"No, of course, I don't."

"You said you were going to look out for her. You told me you'd tell me if anything was going on with her." Jill should have known better than to rely on someone else for something this important.

"I've been telling her she needed to tell you," he said.

"Why didn't *you* tell me?" It hurt to think that, once again, Rachel had confided in Grant rather than her mother. "I *trusted* you."

Grant sat down on the edge of the bed and looked up at her. "I didn't think it was my place. Her relationship isn't related to her health."

"Are you kidding me?" Jill was incredulous. How could he be so ignorant? "Of course it is. How can she have a relationship with someone else when she hasn't even come to terms herself with everything she's lost because of this disease? She needs to be mentally strong to keep up the fight. What's going to happen when it all falls apart? When this Austin leaves her?"

"You don't know it's going to fall apart." He walked over to her. "Look, Jill, isn't it just possible that the reason you're focusing so hard on protecting Rachel is so that you don't have to move on with your own life?"

How dare he!

There was no point trying to talk to him about this. She walked into the bathroom to calm down. She rinsed her face and stared into the mirror. Who was this woman who'd just made love to someone she'd known only a few months? She'd allowed this to happen—encouraged him, even. First kissing him and then asking him to bring her to his place after the dance. He had been so loving, both passionate and tender.

He was wrong about her. She had been prepared to move on with her own life. Tonight had proven that. She squeezed her eyes closed to try to stop the pain of his betrayal—and Rachel's. They'd kept secrets from her. Important secrets. How did someone move on from that?

"I'm going home," she said as she emerged from the bathroom.

"I'll drive you."

"No. I'll call a taxi. I don't want to spend even five minutes more with you."

GRANT WATCHED the taxi's tail lights disappear around the corner. She'd stood outside, in the chilly middle of the night, for thirty minutes waiting for that damn cab. That's how much Jill hated him.

He'd stuck his foot in it big time. Rachel was probably going to be pissed with him, too. Well, she shouldn't have been keeping secrets from her mother. That was the problem with secrets. They led to lies. His ex had taught him that.

Grant strode to the kitchen, picked up each of the half-drunk glasses of Pinot Grigio and downed them one after the other. *No point letting it go to waste.* Then he grabbed the bottle and wandered into the living room.

He put the bottle to his lips and swallowed heavily. It would never replace his Lagavulin.

His mother had taught him to be considerate of guests, so he'd asked Rachel what her mother liked to drink. Now he had a half-case of the wine in the cellar that he had to figure out what to do with. It wasn't like he'd ever be able to share Jill's wine with another woman.

Why not? They'd only had one night together. Wasn't that his usual operating procedure? No strings. No commitments. Have some fun and then move on. Of course, usually the terms were mutually agreed upon—both parties knowing the parameters before they began. He'd foolishly forgotten that step with Jill.

Except he hadn't forgotten, had he? He'd known from the beginning that she wasn't that kind of woman. Hadn't he told himself he needed to keep away from her?

So why was he upset that she was using Rachel's illness as an excuse not to move on with her own life? It wasn't like he was in a position to be a part of her future. But heaven knew, he'd wanted her. Still did. He took another pull on the bottle. It was good that she hated him. Then she'd stay away. Obviously, he couldn't be trusted to do the right thing where she was concerned.

EIGHT

Somehow, Jill had managed to fall asleep after she'd returned home in the early hours of the morning. She awoke groggily to find the pot of coffee Rachel made had gone cold because she had slept in far later than the programmable hotplate allowed. Rachel had left a note saying she'd gone out with friends and would be home late.

Friends? Friend? *Austin.*

Rachel had been sleeping soundly when Jill checked on her. There'd been a couple of telephone messages posted on the refrigerator door—including one from Mae—so her daughter had obviously been home last evening rather than sneaking around with her boyfriend while Jill was out with Grant.

Okay, so maybe Jill had overreacted. A lot. She shuddered at the memory.

Why had she done it? Was Grant right and she was using Rachel's illness as an excuse to push him away? It had been so long since she'd thought of herself as anything but a wife and mother, she'd forgotten what it felt like to be a woman—to feel the pull of attraction to a man and know he was feeling the same way.

Grant had called her beautiful. They'd made love and it was wonderful. The things he'd done to her...what she'd done to him...

What would Calvin think?

The thought came to her suddenly. It hadn't even been two years since he'd died and she'd already been intimate with another man.

But Calvin *had* died. He'd left her all alone to deal with Rachel's illness, and with a lifetime to remember all the dreams they'd never realize. She massaged her temples. Still, that was no reason to throw herself at Grant like a wanton woman. She was no different than that Mary-something from the dance.

She buried her face in her hands. Last night had been thrilling. Jill had wholeheartedly embraced thoughts of a new life...a new man. But in the harsh light of day, she felt off-kilter, unable to recognize the woman who had laughed and danced and made love with Grant.

Why couldn't she let go of her past? Of Calvin and Rachel, and who she'd been with them? How could Rachel find it so easy to move on?

Austin. The name ground into Jill's psyche like a pebble lodged in a shoe, growing more irritating with every step. She needed to talk to Rachel about him—about why she'd kept him secret—but she wasn't up for a big dramatic argument.

She might leave, a small voice cautioned. *She has somewhere else she could go to now, someone else to turn to*. No, this discussion would require special care.

She picked up the phone and called the one person she knew she could talk to about this…

JILL SLID into the familiar booth at the back of Ollee's, away from the pool tables. Because it was the middle of the afternoon, the popular local restaurant and bar was almost empty. Only a few die-hard regulars had turned out to shoot a few balls and grab a beer to cap off the weekend.

Sally, the long-time waitress, put a glass of Pinot Grigio on the table in front of her. "Anything to eat, hon?"

"Yeah," Jill said. She wasn't particularly hungry, but it would be bad to drink on an empty stomach. "I'll have a chicken quesadilla."

Jill took a sip of her wine and then wandered over to the jukebox to see if anything new had been added to the rotation. A lot of country songs about cheating lovers and broken hearts. Not what she wanted to hear at this particular moment.

"Well, hello there, sweetie." Mae wrapped an arm around Jill and peered at the jukebox list. "See anything you like?"

"Not really." Jill turned to hug her friend. "I'm sorry it took so long for us to get together."

"Well, we're together now, so let's have a time of it." Mae motioned to Sally at the bar. "I'll just be a sec," she said to Jill and went over to the bar to chat with the waitress.

Jill envied Mae. In her mid-seventies, she had the energy of someone half her age. Her grey hair was chopped short and she wore it spikey in a way that would have looked ridiculous on most older women. She loved makeup, bright colours, and big jewellery. She was like a steamroller when she wanted to get something done, and she had the biggest, most generous heart of anyone Jill had ever met.

"Here we are." Mae slid into the booth across from Jill and raised a glass of something that wasn't her usual bourbon. "To us," she said, tapping her glass against Jill's.

"To us," Jill repeated. "Are you trying out a new drink today?"

Mae laughed. "It's plain ole orange juice, sweetie. Not as fresh as what I grew up with in Georgia, but a ray of sunshine from home, all the same."

Mae didn't say anything as Jill expressed her concerns about Rachel returning to school and how betrayed she felt by her daughter's attempt to hide her relationship with Austin. "Doesn't she understand how vulnerable she is right now?" Jill pushed away the half-eaten quesadilla and used her napkin to wipe the tears that were stinging her eyes.

"Oh, sweetie." Mae reached across the table and took her hands. "I know you're scared for her. You're her momma and you're always gonna worry. But you can't keep her locked up like a fragile princess. She wants to go out and experience life—probably even more now, after the cancer, than before. She's got a real appreciation of just how precious and precarious life is."

"What if they didn't get it all and it comes back, or if it spread to some other part of her body? What if she gets sick again?" Only to Mae could she express her true fears for Rachel.

Mae smiled sadly. "Then you'd be happy she got all the livin' in she could while she was feelin' well. That will make her all the stronger to fight again."

"Another drink, ladies?" Sally asked.

"No, I think I'd better switch to coffee." Jill was starting to feel the first twinges of a caffeine-deprived headache coming on.

"Hit me again, darlin'." Mae handed Sally her glass.

"So, what do I do?" Jill asked.

"Nothin'. If she thinks she's ready to return to school, you let her. And she'll tell you about her new beau when she thinks the time is right. Sweetie, you need to stop focusin' on Rachel's life and start livin' your own."

Jill rolled her eyes. Mae was starting to sound like Rachel—and Grant for that matter. Didn't they understand that her daughter was all she had left now?

"I heard you were out with Dr. Delicious last night," Mae said.

She should have known Rachel would blab to Mae about where she was. "I don't want to talk about it."

"Okay." Mae leaned back in her seat and waited.

For the first time since she'd arrived, Jill took a close look at her friend. Dark circles shadowed her eyes. Her cheeks had hollowed and her complexion appeared greyish under her heavy makeup. *And she's not drinking.*

"How are things with you?" Jill tried to keep her voice light to hide a gnawing fear. Hopefully, Mae had simply drunk too much the night before and was hungover. But what if it was something else?

Mae eyed her for a few seconds and then leaned forward. "Well, there's no way to sugar coat this, sweetie. The cancer's back."

Jill felt the floor disappear from beneath her and she was plummeting down a long dark tunnel. "Oh, Mae!"

"Now, just stop right there! I've beaten this thing twice before and I'm goin' for—what do they call it in hockey?—a hat trick. I've got my support team in place and you know if I need reinforcements, you're top of my call list. I just wanted you to know, in case you needed me and I wasn't able to get to you right away."

Top of her call list. Jill was devastated. Mae had been trying to get together with her for weeks and Jill had kept putting her off. And yet, as soon as Jill needed her, Mae was right there for her. "I'm so sorry, Mae," Jill whispered. "For the cancer, but also for not being there when you needed me. You've been such a good friend to me and I've—"

"All right, enough with the pity-party. You want to make it up to me, sweetie? You tell me about you and the delectable Dr. Palmer. I need to have something to chew on while I'm at my appointments next week."

"There's nothing to tell."

"Don't play shy, sweetie. Your words say *non, non, non,* but your blushing cheeks say *oui, oui, oui.*"

"Okay." Jill couldn't help but laugh at Mae's comical expression and Georgia-affected French accent. She told her everything: from her arrival at the clinic with the raccoon to Sherlock and her kiss, to the firemen's dance and making love, to her argument with Grant about Austin, and her concern that she'd been disloyal to Calvin's memory. "Rachel was diagnosed almost immediately after Calvin died. She's been my sole focus ever since. How can I have feelings for Grant if I've never even had the opportunity to mourn my husband?"

"That's a very good question." Mae had seemed to thoroughly enjoy hearing all the details about Grant but now turned serious. "I know you hold yourself responsible for Calvin's death, but if you look deep in your heart, you know there was nothin' you could have done for him that night."

"I could have been there."

"True enough, but there's no guarantee that things would have turned out any differently if you had been. CPR is all well and good, but when death comes knockin' we can't lock the door. You can't save everyone, but you were there for Rachel when she needed you." She reached across the table and grasped Jill's hands. "People mourn in different ways, sweetie. Perhaps takin' care of Rachel was your way of mournin' for Calvin."

Jill closed her eyes. At one time, the thought of her husband's death had brought a pain that was searing and raw. Their life, their dreams, their future was gone. They had put off too much, always waiting for a time that never came. But you only have the present, she knew that now. There was so much in the past that she regretted not doing, but that gut-wrenching hurt was gone. Now, she felt sadness for a life that was cut too short, and grief for all that Calvin would miss. When had that happened?

"There comes a time when you have to stop grieving and start livin' again." Mae took a napkin and wiped away Jill's tears. "Maybe now is that time."

NINE

Man, would this day ever be over?

Grant glanced at his watch. Lately, the days seemed to drag in a way he couldn't ever remember happening before.

It had been more than a week since his disastrous date with Jill. She hadn't come to the clinic—not even to check on Sherlock. He supposed Rachel could be keeping her updated on the dog's miraculous recovery, but then again…Rachel had been acting strangely, too.

He'd expected Rachel to come into the office Monday morning ready to tear a strip off him for telling her mother about Austin, but she hadn't said a word about it. She seemed distant, though. Something was up with her.

Loretta had called last night to invite him to a birthday dinner for one of the boys—and, of course, to bring Jill along. He'd made some stupid excuse for not going, but he hadn't fooled his sister-in-law. She gave him an earful about how terrific Jill was—as if he didn't already know—and what an idiot he would be if he allowed his bad experience with Nancy—although she'd used a more colourful name for his ex—as an excuse to avoid commitment. Loretta wasn't shy about expressing her opinions.

A dozen times or more he'd almost called Jill. Once he'd actually dialled the phone, but he'd hung up before the first ring. What would he have said to her anyway?

Rachel poked her head into his office. "Our last patient just cancelled, so I'm off."

"Wait," Grant said. "Do you have a minute?"

"Sure." Rachel stepped into the office and closed the door. "What's up?"

"I wanted to ask you the same thing." He took a breath. "Have I done something to upset you?"

She seemed taken aback by the question. "No. I wish things had worked out with you and my mom, but…" She shrugged.

He did, too, but it was for the best—at least that's what he kept telling himself. "It's just that you seem a little distant, lately."

"Oh, sorry. We got some bad news about Mae Pruitt. Her cancer returned and I guess it kind of bummed me out."

"Mae?" His heart sank. "I didn't know. I'm very sorry to hear that."

"Well, you know what a fighter she is. I think she'll be okay. It threw Mom for a spin, though. Just when I thought she was ready to let me go, she seems to be holding on even tighter." Rachel cocked her head and grinned. "You don't want to try again with her, do you?"

Oh, boy. Minefield.

"Sorry, that wasn't fair of me. I know Mom's not ready to move on yet," she said quickly. "Anyway, you'll be happy to know that I'm going to tell her about Austin tonight. I've invited him to dinner. Wish me luck."

After Rachel left, Grant wandered over to Sherlock's pen and released him. He'd been allowing the dog to spend the night in his home. It was good for the animal and he liked the company.

Stop it. At least be honest with yourself. Sherlock was a reminder of Jill and, in some sick way, having the dog with him made her feel close. Like she didn't hate his guts.

He'd also finished about half the bottles of Pinot.

He should just call her, try to work things out between them.

And then what?

He wanted her. There was no denying that. When he closed his eyes he could picture her glowing face, feel her soft skin beneath his fingers, the scent of her, the taste of her... It never left him.

But he also missed the way she challenged him, made him think about his beliefs. He even missed her crazy passion for taking on lost-cause animals. But most of all, he missed her laughter. He'd loved making her laugh.

Sherlock was moving well, now. The paralysis in his leg was almost totally reversed. There was no reason for him to remain at the clinic. He needed to go to a home where he'd be well taken care of by someone with the energy and passion to follow-through on the prescribed exercise and rehabilitation regime. The Simmonses, realizing their limitations, had surrendered him to Jill.

Grant picked up the phone and dialled her number. He listened to the answering machine, hung up, and dialled again—just to hear her voice. This time he left a message asking Jill what she wanted to do about Sherlock.

It wasn't a ploy to talk to her—to get her to talk to him—Jill was officially responsible for the Beagle.

You just keep telling yourself that this thing with Jill can be just business and, maybe with time, you'll actually believe it.

JILL IGNORED the ringing telephone to focus on the man standing in front of her. "This is Austin," Rachel had said as if it was the most natural thing in the world that she would bring this person to their home without any forewarning.

Jill had taken Mae's advice and said nothing about knowing Rachel was seeing someone. She should be thrilled that her daughter had finally decided to tell her about him. But she'd expected a conversation not an introduction.

He wasn't quite how she'd pictured him. He was tall and slim with reddish-brown hair and a neatly trimmed beard. She suspected he wore the beard to look older because his skin was porcelain-smooth and he had a youthful air about him. He wore glasses, round silver wired spectacles that exaggerated the size of his hazel-coloured eyes. He looked presentable enough in black dress pants and an olive-green golf shirt.

"It's a pleasure to meet you, Mrs. Bennett." His voice was far deeper than she'd expected from someone so young.

"*Finally.*" She hadn't meant to sound quite so petulant.

He grinned at her. He had good teeth. "Yes, finally." He turned to Rachel with an I-told-you-so look, which warmed Jill's chilly attitude by a few degrees.

"I wasn't expecting company for dinner. I'm not sure we have enough. Maybe you should come back another time?"

"Mom, really?" Rachel placed her hands on her hips and jutted out her chin in a manner Jill recognized as an imitation of her own defiant gesture. "I think we have enough food in the house that we can come up with something to feed all of us."

"I'd be happy to help." Austin's gaze shifted back and forth between Jill and Rachel.

"He's a really good cook." Rachel's expression softened when she looked at him. She turned back to Jill. "Why don't you pour yourself a glass of wine and let us make you dinner."

"I could make you a special cocktail. Tell me what flavours you like and I can create one just for you."

"Oh yeah, he does it all the time at The Ceeps. It's, like, his specialty."

Jill took a bottle of wine from the refrigerator. "I like grapes."

She was relentless during dinner, digging through Austin's past and quizzing him about his employment prospects. She was reminded of Calvin's reaction to the first boy Rachel had ever brought home. Jill had chastised her husband for trying to scare him away through intimidation. Now, she was doing the same.

Austin, however, didn't seem intimidated by her interrogation, and aside from some eye-rolling and the occasional "why would you ask that?" Rachel didn't seem perturbed by it, either. The two of them presented a united front, often laughing at each other's responses. Occasionally, Austin would take Rachel's hand and lift it to his lips, particularly if she'd just come to his defence. "Your mom is only worried about you," he'd say to her.

As much as she fought it, Jill found herself liking this young man more than she wanted to. It wasn't only his openness and easy charm, it was the loving way he looked at Rachel even when he didn't think Jill was watching. And more importantly, it was the glow of happiness that radiated from her daughter.

"We'll do the dishes," Rachel said, rising from the table.

Jill wandered into the living room. Finnegan and Joss trotted along behind her. Okay, so Austin seemed like a good guy, and he seemed to sincerely care for Rachel. But that didn't mean their relationship was a good thing.

"Mrs. Bennett." Austin stood in the entryway. "I brought you a cup of tea. I thought maybe we could talk, just the two of us."

Tea? She'd rather have another glass of wine, but she'd had three already and was feeling a little light-headed. Was it that obvious? She looked up at him. Oh, right. He was a bartender, trained to recognize the signs of intoxication. "Thank you." She took the cup from him and motioned for him to sit. Sacha had been sleeping on the loveseat beside Jill. He now rose, stretched, and hopped over to Austin's lap.

Traitor.

"I can imagine how worried you are about Rachel," he said, shifting the cat to a more comfortable position. "I want to assure you that I will do my best to take care of her. I love her."

"How can you know you love her? You only met a short time ago. And I don't think you understand her situation."

"She's been honest with me about her treatment and prognosis."

"Really?" Jill took a sip of tea and eyed him over the cup. "Do you like kids?"

"Of course. Love them. That's why I went into teaching."

"You've probably always dreamed of having a houseful of them, haven't you?" Jill didn't wait for a response. "So how would you feel knowing you and Rachel can never have any?"

"Mom!" Rachel stood in the doorway, her hands covering her face.

Austin held out his hand to her. "It's okay, she's just worried about you." Rachel came to him and sat down on the arm of his chair. He turned back to Jill. "I imagine I feel the same way you feel about not ever being a grandmother to her children."

Jill hadn't expected that.

"I love Rachel and she loves me." The look he gave Rachel was so warm and accepting, Jill felt like a voyeur. "Yes, I know we can never have children of our own, but that doesn't mean we can't be parents. There are a lot of kids out there who need a good home. Would you love a child any less because it didn't have Rachel's DNA?"

"No, of course not."

"Me neither."

"Me neither," Rachel added, smiling down at him.

Jill was surprised that they had talked about adopting children. She had done quite a bit of research in anticipation of raising the subject with Rachel when the time was right, but she'd always felt it was too soon in her daughter's recovery. Apparently not.

"What about Rachel's plan to move to Guelph in a few months?" Jill wondered how this new relationship fit in with her daughter's plans to return to school. Perhaps, she could enlist Austin's help in persuading Rachel to delay it.

"Austin's already been in touch with the school board there about getting his name on the supply teaching list," Rachel said.

"And I've got a good reference from The Ceeps, so I can pick up a bartending job to help pay the bills until I get hired on full-time," he added.

"Wait a minute!" The teacup shook in her hand and Jill put it down on the side table before it spilled. She stared at the two of them. "You're planning on moving to Guelph *together*?"

"Of course. I don't want her to go by herself. I'd be afraid she'd get so engrossed in her school work that she'd forget to eat properly and get enough sleep. She's doing great, but she's only just finished her treatment."

Exactly the same concerns Jill had.

"Look, Mom, we don't know what the future holds for us—none of us do. But I do know that Austin and I love each other." Rachel slid down onto Austin's lap, displacing Sacha, who meowed and jumped down. "Life is risky. You never know what it's going to throw at you. You know that better than anyone."

Austin wrapped his arms around Rachel. "Are we moving quickly? Yes. Are we scared? Maybe a little. But I know when I get up in the morning, Rachel is my first thought. When I go to sleep, she's my last. I don't want to waste any time we might have."

Jill leaned back against the loveseat. Mae had said pretty much the same thing when Jill had worried that

Rachel's cancer would come back. *Then you'd be happy she got all the livin' in she could while she was feelin' well. That will make her all the stronger to fight again.*

"You have given me a gift," Rachel said, moving to sit down on the loveseat beside Jill. "It's because of you I have my life back. It's because of you, Austin and I can plan a future together. But it needs to be *my* life. It can't be yours." She took Jill's hands. "I love you, Mom, and I will always need you, but right now, I need you to loosen your grip, just a bit, for both our sakes."

Jill nodded, eyes glistening with unshed tears, and embraced her daughter. It was the first time in months that Rachel had allowed her to hug her for more than a few seconds. She was surprised by how strong and firm she felt. She'd put on weight, and her hair was getting a little longer—long enough, anyway, that Jill could see its colour had changed from dark auburn to a golden brown. Another change marking Rachel's independence from Jill. It suited her, though. "Okay." She swallowed the lump in her throat. "I'll try."

"That's all I'm asking," Rachel whispered and kissed her cheek.

The house was quiet after Rachel and Austin left. Jill hadn't even asked what time her daughter would be home. She was an adult. They were past that now.

Austin loved her daughter, and Jill believed him when he said he would take care of her. For the first time, in almost two years, she didn't have to bear the weight of Rachel's cancer alone. She had an ally.

But even as the weight of caring for Rachel lifted from her shoulders, a familiar hollowness filled the pit of her stomach.

In the days following Calvin's death, Jill had been terrified of what would become of her. They'd been together for so long, she hadn't known how to live without him. But then Rachel had gotten sick and she'd thrown herself into caring for her daughter. Now that Rachel no longer needed her, Jill could feel the black emptiness engulfing her again.

There comes a time, when you have to stop grieving and start livin' again, Mae had said.

Jill took a deep breath and the dark hole got a little smaller. She continued breathing deeply, Mae's words repeating over and over in her mind. Gradually, the panic subsided.

Mae was right. Maybe that time was now.

TEN

No one should look that amazing first thing on a Sunday morning.

Surprise, relief, and then out-and-out lust waved through Grant as he drank in the vision of Jill standing on his doorstep.

The morning sunlight highlighted her auburn hair, making her curls appear like a halo. She was dressed more casually than he'd ever seen, in snug blue jeans that hugged her hips—*lucky jeans*—and a brown leather and sheepskin jacket that hung open to reveal a russet-coloured sweater with a boat-neck collar. The stiletto heels on her brown suede ankle boots gave her a good three inches on him, which he found highly erotic. Her cheeks were flushed, but he couldn't tell whether it was from the cool morning air or if she'd applied a light dusting of blush. Regardless, she looked poised and confident, and sexy as hell.

"You're here about Sherlock, I suppose," he said, scratching his freshly shaved chin. He'd quickly thrown on a pair of jeans and an old London Knights hockey jersey to answer the door.

Jill's eyes widened and she took a step back. "No. What about Sherlock? Is he okay?"

"You didn't get my message?" If she wasn't here about Sherlock, why had she come? "I called last night."

"Oh, sorry. I heard the phone, but then completely forgot to check the message. It was a busy night. Rachel introduced me to Austin." She sheepishly looked down at her feet. "I came to—Oh, my goodness! Sherlock!" Jill squatted and hugged the Beagle who'd appeared at Grant's side. "Look at you. Oh, you beautiful boy. My beautiful boy."

With her head buried deep in Sherlock's neck and her voice muffled, Grant couldn't tell if she was laughing or crying. Still, he felt a ridiculous sense of pride in the dog's recovery. He was always amazed at the resilience of animals to survive adversity. It helped, of course, that Sherlock didn't know that the surgery wasn't supposed to have been as successful as it was, or that his paralysis shouldn't be almost totally reversed. The self-awareness humans possessed could be beneficial in helping them recover from a catastrophic event, but it could also be detrimental if they believed their prognosis to be poor.

"How can I ever thank you?" Jill's face glowed with joy as tears streamed down her cheeks.

Several possibilities popped into his head—all of them having to do with Jill being naked. Man, he was a jerk. She was sincerely grateful to him for helping the dog, and all he could think about was carrying her into his bedroom and making love with her over and over again.

He wiped a tear from her cheek and then pulled her to

her feet. "Do you want to come in for a cup of coffee? We need to talk about what's next for Sherlock."

She nodded, rubbed away the remaining tears from her cheeks, and brushed past him.

Set her up with a rehabilitation specialist and let her go. Grant repeated the sentence to himself several times as he followed her into the kitchen. She's not ready for anything else. That's what Rachel had said. And besides, it wasn't as if he wanted a relationship, anyway. It was just that she was so, so sexy… The way her ass moved in those jeans.

Jill had hung her jacket on the back of one of the chairs, taken down two mugs from the cupboard, and poured the coffee. He was struck by how right it felt to have her in his kitchen, how she knew where he kept things, how she handed him a mug as if it was the most natural thing in the world. It felt good to have her there, to see her smile, to know she didn't detest him.

Knock it off, Palmer. It's a cup of coffee not a freakin' Nobel Peace Prize.

His attempt to appear *blasé* toward her comfort in his kitchen was ruined when he took too large a sip and burned his tongue on the piping hot liquid. "Oww!"

"Are you okay?"

"Yeah, fine." He put his cup down. "So, if you didn't get my message about Sherlock, why are you here?"

"Oh." Her cheeks glowed with embarrassment and she chewed her bottom lip, hesitating. "I came here to apologize. I said some awful things to you after…when we…" She took a shaky breath. "The last time I was here."

She looked absolutely adorable in her discomfort.

Jill winced. "Anyway, I just wanted to tell you that I'm sorry."

"It's not your fault," Grant said. "I shouldn't have let things go as far as they did. It hasn't been that long since you lost your husband, and with what you've been through with Rachel, well… I should have known it was too soon for you." He took a deep breath and regretted the words before he even uttered them. "I promise, it won't happen again."

"Oh! Well, that's too bad."

What? Had he heard her correctly? "What did you say?"

Her face flamed red. "Nothing. I'm just being silly."

He gazed into her eyes, trying to read her mind, ignoring the voice in his head that was yelling at him to *JUST LET HER GO*.

"I mean, it was just one night. It's not like it was a big deal or anything. We're both adults." She hugged her arms against her chest and her voice rose in both pitch and pace. "I mean, I'm sure it was nothing to you. You must have lots of girlfriends—do this all the time, right?"

Did she think so little of him? "When we first met you called me a monster. Should I be happy that I've been promoted to heartless gigolo?"

"No, that's not what I meant." She sank onto one of the kitchen chairs and buried her head in her hands. The poised, confident woman who had appeared at his front door was gone. Sherlock nudged her leg and she dropped one arm to assure him she was all right. "I'm making a mess of this."

"But you *do* think I'm in the habit of seducing women?" His voice was hard.

"Well, I don't think I'm the first woman you've slept

with since your wife left you. Probably not even the second, or third." Jill raised her head, her eyes challenging him to deny it.

True enough. Grant wasn't sure why he was so offended by her assertion. Hadn't he already determined that this was the precise reason he needed to keep his distance from Jill?

Yet, it wasn't her censure about the number of women he'd been with that infuriated him, but rather her contention that she had been nothing more than another notch on his bedpost—that somehow, she hadn't been any different than the others.

Oh, crap! The realization of hit him hard. He turned and stalked out of the kitchen. Now, what was he going to do?

"Grant, wait!"

He turned back.

"I'm sorry. I didn't mean to upset you. Darn it, I keep saying the wrong things."

"What are you trying to say?" He held out his hand and led her into the living room. When she chose to sit on the couch, he selected the armchair opposite. Even the brief touch of her fingers had ignited a fire deep within him. He couldn't imagine trying to have a conversation with her while sitting thigh-to-thigh.

Sherlock rested his cheek on the couch and Jill lifted him up beside her.

Grant frowned.

"Oh, sorry." She gave Sherlock a conspiratorial scratch behind the ears. "I bet you don't let the animals up on your furniture, do you?"

"Not usually."

"Furniture is for people, right?"

"Exactly."

She smiled mischievously and his heart softened as he realized she was teasing him about their differences of opinion concerning the role and treatment of animals. It was what had brought them together in the first place.

"Austin is planning on moving to Guelph with Rachel," Jill said.

"Are you okay with that?"

"Surprisingly, yes. I think it will be good for her to put the cancer behind her and resume her life."

"What about you? Can you put her cancer behind you?"

"I don't think I will ever stop worrying about her," Jill conceded. "But there's nothing more I can do for her. I have to stop focusing on her and decide what I want to do with my life."

"And what is that?"

"I don't know, for sure, but I do know that I want to take more risks. Everything with Calvin was about planning for the future—a future that never came. And even while I was caring for Rachel, and I felt I was living day-to-day, I was really only focused on forcing a positive outcome—always worrying about what I had to do at the moment to make sure she'd be okay tomorrow. I don't want to live like that anymore. I *can't* live like that anymore."

Grant was mesmerized by the motion of Jill's hand as it gently ran along the length of Sherlock's back. Suddenly, she stopped and snapped her fingers. Startled, he looked up at her face.

"Are you listening to me?" she asked impatiently.

"I don't know what you're asking. What do you mean you want to take more risks? Are you talking about skydiving? Changing jobs? Moving to Bali?"

She sighed in exasperation. "Do you find me attractive? I mean, I think you do, the way you always watch my butt when I walk."

He thought he'd been subtler than that. "Of course, I do."

"Enough that, despite what you said before, you'd want to make love to me again?"

"Jill, what are you asking of me?"

She stood and came to stand directly in front of him, forcing Grant to crane his neck to look up at her. She was magnificent. "I'm asking if the night of the firemen's dance was a one-time thing or whether you'd like to do it, again?"

Grant pulled her down onto his lap and kissed her desperately. He hadn't thought he'd taste her sweet lips again. She strained against him, so warm and soft, so perfect.

"Oh good, I'll take that as a 'yes,'" Jill said throatily against his cheek when she paused to catch her breath.

Grant shuddered and forced himself to pull back. He gazed into those lovely whiskey eyes, darkened now with passion. He wanted her more than anything, but he needed to be honest with her. "I'm crazy about you, Jill. Heck, I'm probably three-quarters in love with you. But I just don't know that I can give you what you want."

She stroked his cheek. "How can you possibly know what I want when I don't even know what I want?"

"I just assumed you wanted something permanent, some sort of commitment."

She shrugged. "Maybe in time. I'm forty-four years old and I've only ever been with one other man—my husband. I'm not sure I even know how to be with someone else, so there's no way I'd ask for a commitment from you when I'm not even sure I can make one myself."

He hadn't expected that. It was exhilarating and a little disconcerting, too. He should be relieved that she wasn't pressing him for more but instead, he found himself wanting her to be certain of him, wanting to be certain of her.

"Can we just see where things lead without doing any planning or too much thinking?" she asked. "I'd like to take the time to just *be* together. I've never done that before, and I'd like to try it—with you."

"I have a confession to make." He grinned at her. "I lied before. I am one hundred percent in love with you."

"*Finally* something we can agree on." Jill wrapped her arms tightly around his neck and gazed deeply into his eyes. "Because I'm one hundred percent in love with you, too."

"I'll bet I can find something else we can agree on," Grant grinned wickedly as he gently pulled Jill's head toward his and kissed her deeply.

EPILOGUE

Jill stood at the window, waving until the rental van disappeared in the blowing snow. She tried not to focus too much on the trenches its tires had dug into the twelve centimetres of snow that had fallen since midnight. Rachel was off to begin her new adventure in Guelph. Austin was with her, she'd be fine.

They had sublet a small apartment just off-campus. It wasn't great, but it would do for now. Austin had been offered a temporary teaching position, filling in for a maternity leave, beginning next month. He was hopeful it was the first step to a more permanent position with the local school board. It certainly paid better than tending bar and meant he'd be home evenings.

Jill turned away from the window and wandered through the quiet house. She'd miss Rachel terribly, but Guelph was only a few hours away.

"Are you sure there's nothing else you want to take?" Grant met her in the hallway.

She shook her head and stepped into his arms. "I'm

sure. I've got everything that has sentimental value. The auctioneers can deal with the rest."

He kissed her cheek and she snuggled closer. So much for their commitment-free relationship. They'd been together only a week before Grant had asked her to move in with him once Rachel left for school. She hadn't hesitated. It just felt right.

Rachel had been enthusiastic about Jill's planned change in accommodation, encouraging her and Grant not to wait. Jill suspected she'd wanted her out of the house sooner, so she could move Austin in before they left for Guelph. But that wasn't going to happen. Jill was okay with Rachel and Austin living together in Guelph. She wasn't okay with it under Calvin's roof. She fully acknowledged she was being old-fashioned—especially since she was planning to move in with Grant—but she still thought of the home as hers and Calvin's, and she knew her husband wouldn't have approved.

"I guess that's it, then," Grant said. "Do you want a moment?"

Jill looked over Grant's shoulder into the living room and then down the hallway to the entrance of the kitchen. She didn't need to walk through the rooms again. Every nook and cranny of this home was etched into her heart. She had been happy here. She'd had a wonderful husband and they'd raised a beautiful daughter. She would never forget.

She wouldn't stay mired in the past, either. Calvin wouldn't have wanted her to. It was time to start her new life, with another wonderful man, and build happy memories with him.

She kissed Grant and stepped back. "No, we should get

going. I promised Mae we'd stop in for a quick visit after we got Rachel off."

Mae, her beautiful, brave friend, was battling on. She'd just finished her first round of radiation and the doctors were pleased with her progress. Of course, anyone who knew Mae was not the least bit surprised. Her oldest grandson was graduating high school in June and she was determined to attend his commencement ceremony.

They stepped out on the porch. Jill locked the door and pocketed the key. Out of the corner of her eye, she saw the scrawny, ragged tabby cat that had been lurking in the neighbourhood for the past few weeks. Several times she'd left food out for it, and once she'd managed to pet it before it took off, startled by one of the dog's barking.

She reached into her purse and pulled out a package of dried liver she kept for animal treats. She shook the package and bent down, calling softly to the cat.

Grant glared at her over the hood of his SUV. "Jill?" he called, cautiously. "What are you doing?"

"Shhh, you'll scare him." She stayed very still as the cat approached. No dogs to worry about today, only a big scary vet with a bad attitude. She glanced up at Grant who was shaking his head in dismay.

The cat began purring as soon as she picked him up. He was nothing but skin and bones and shivering from the cold, poor thing. She carried him to the car.

"What are you going to do with that?" Grant asked.

"Feed him, to start with," she said, opening the door and sliding into the passenger seat.

"You can't bring him into the house. He probably has

fleas. He'll infest the rest of the menagerie you've brought over."

"Then we'll take him to the clinic and get him checked out first."

"Who do you think is going to do that?" Grant's eyebrows rose.

"I know this very sexy veterinarian…" She winked at him.

Grant gave an exaggerated sigh as he closed her door. "You know you can't save them all, right?" He got into the vehicle.

"I know," Jill leaned over and kissed his cheek. Their time together had confirmed for her that Grant wasn't nearly as hard-hearted as he liked to pretend. He held free monthly spay and neuter clinics for pets of homeless people and offered his services to the local humane society. "But we can help the ones in our little corner of the world."

"Why do I get the feeling your corner of the world is not so little?" Grant started the engine and backed down the driveway.

Jill smiled to herself. She hadn't heard the end of it, but that was one of the things she loved most about Grant. They both felt free to speak their minds. They could—and did—disagree passionately about many things, but always made up just as passionately as they argued.

This life was so different from the one she'd known before. But it was good, and Jill was happy. She had found true love twice, and both were forever.

What's next in the **Seasons of Love** series? How about a Christmas romance?

Seven years ago Monica Stevens left her home town with no intention of returning. Her inability to conceive a child not only devastated her fifteen-year marriage, it made her doubt her appeal as a woman. When her mother has to undergo surgery, she reluctantly agrees to come back to run the Mother Goose Daycare until she's recovered.

Luke McMillan is struggling to balance his career with his duties as a single father to six adopted children. The death of his wife has thrown the adoption of his two youngest sons into limbo. He is further stymied by a dogmatic social worker who questions whether a single parent can adequately care for so many kids.

Initially brought together by the children, Monica and Luke quickly surrender to their growing passion. But when she learns about the threatened adoption, Monica wonders if Luke's interest in her is only as a mother to his children. Is history about to repeat itself, or will a Christmas miracle finally give Monica the family she's always dreamed of having?

Pre-order Six Geese for Monica today to find out whether six little geese can create a Christmas miracle. (Available November 18, 2025)

You can stay up-to-date on upcoming releases, giveaways, sales and all sorts of shenanigans by joining my newsletter, *The Gayle Gazette*.

Sign up at brendagayle.com.

If you enjoyed *Twice & Forever*, please let your friends know so they can experience the relationship of Jill and Grant as well. If you leave a review on your favourite retailer, book site, or your own blog, I'd love to read it. Email me the link at brenda@brendagayle.com.

Are you looking for something a little different? How about a historical mystery series set in post-World War II Kingston, Ontario?

She's a reporter with a nose for trouble.
But when the story is murder, will she end up above the fold or get buried in the back?

Check out all six books in the Charley Hall Historical Mystery series.

A NOTE FROM THE AUTHOR

Ovarian cancer is a terrible disease, affecting thousands of women and their families every year. Still, only 2.1% of donations for cancer are directed toward ovarian cancer. With these limited funds, organizations such as Ovarian Cancer Canada are providing support, education, and research. While there has been some progress in treating it, there is a long way to go to ensure a woman diagnosed with ovarian cancer has a similar outcome to women with other cancers.

Inform your friends, your family, and yourself about ovarian cancer. And if you are able, please consider donating your time and/or money to support the fight to eradicate this deadly disease.

TWICE & FOREVER BOOK CLUB DISCUSSION GUIDE

Title: Twice & Forever (Seasons of Love – Autumn)
Author: Brenda Gayle
Genre: Contemporary Women's Fiction / Romance
Setting: Small-town Ontario, Canada

1. BOOK OVERVIEW

Twice & Forever follows Jill Bennett, a widowed mother still grieving her husband's sudden death while caring for her daughter Rachel, a young cancer survivor. Overprotective and emotionally fragile, Jill clings to Rachel just as Rachel seeks independence and a return to veterinary school. Enter Grant Palmer, a pragmatic yet compassionate veterinarian, who challenges Jill's tendency to hold on too tightly whether to animals, memories, or loved ones. As Jill faces her fears of loss and the possibility of new love, she must decide if she's ready to embrace a "second forever."

2. ABOUT THE AUTHOR

Brenda Gayle writes heartfelt contemporary romances that explore resilience, family, and the courage to risk love again. With a background in journalism and corporate communications, she brings emotional depth and realistic dialogue to her novels. Her Seasons of Love series pairs the turning points of relationships with the rhythms of the seasons, reminding readers that every ending can be the beginning of something new.

3. THEMES & TOPICS

- Second chances at love and life
- Grief, guilt, and the struggle to let go
- The bond between mothers and daughters
- Illness, survivorship, and resilience
- The role of animals as companions and healers
- Finding independence while honouring family ties
- Community support and friendship

4. CHARACTER LIST

Jill Bennett – Protagonist; a widowed mother,

compassionate but overprotective, learning to heal and open her heart again.

Rachel Bennett – Jill's daughter; a cancer survivor eager to reclaim her independence and future as a veterinarian.

Dr. Grant Palmer – Veterinarian; pragmatic, principled, and unexpectedly drawn to Jill despite his own scars.

Mae Pruitt – Jill's friend and confidante; feisty, wise, and a grounding influence.

Doug & Loretta Palmer – Grant's brother and sister-in-law; represent stability, family, and community.

Austin – Rachel's love interest; a young teacher whose presence challenges Jill's ability to let go.

5. DISCUSSION QUESTIONS

1. How did your view of Jill evolve throughout the novel? Did you empathize with her protectiveness, or did you find it stifling?
2. Grant approaches animals with pragmatism and compassion. How does this reflect his approach to human relationships?
3. In what ways does Rachel's determination to return to veterinary school highlight generational conflict between mother and daughter?
4. How does grief affect Jill's decisions and relationships? Where does she grow the most?

5. Mae provides wisdom, humour, and encouragement. How important are friendships like hers in stories of healing?
6. Animals in the story often symbolize love, loss, and resilience. Which animal moment stood out to you most, and why?
7. The novel intertwines illness (Rachel's cancer, Mae's health struggles) with themes of hope. How did these storylines deepen the emotional impact?
8. What role does setting (small-town Ontario, changing seasons) play in shaping the mood and themes?
9. The book title, *Twice & Forever*, suggests lasting love can happen more than once. How do you interpret the meaning of "forever" in Jill's journey?
10. If you were Jill's friend, what advice would you have given her at the beginning of the novel? Would it change by the end?

6. MEMORABLE QUOTES FOR DISCUSSION

"It's not my fault he died, Rachel had said, and she was right. It was Jill's." — Jill's crushing guilt shows how grief can distort reality.

"You hold on too tightly." — Grant's observation becomes the heart of Jill's internal struggle.

"I have to go on with my life, and you have to go on

with yours." — Rachel's declaration underscores the theme of independence and renewal.

"For a monster, I make a pretty mean cup of coffee." — Grant's humour lightens tension, revealing chemistry beneath conflict.

7. SUGGESTED ACTIVITIES

Cupcake & Coffee Social – Inspired by Jill's birthday cupcakes and Grant's coffee, bring sweet treats to your meeting.

Animal Rescue Donation Drive – Collect supplies for a local shelter in honor of Jill's rescues.

Second Chances Sharing Circle – Invite members to share personal stories of second chances in life, love, or career.

Autumn Comfort Night – Celebrate the seasonal theme with pumpkin bread, apple cider, and cozy fall recipes.

8. OTHER BOOKS IN THE SEASONS OF LOVE SERIES

- Six Geese for Monica - Winter
- The Color of You - Spring
- The Parent Trip - Summer

ABOUT BRENDA GAYLE

I've been a writer all my life but returned to my love of fiction after more than 20 years in the world of corporate communications—although some might argue there is plenty of opportunity for fiction-writing there, too. A fan of many genres, I find it hard to stay within the publishing industry's prescribed boxes. Whether it's historical mystery, romantic suspense, or women's fiction, my greatest joy is creating deeply emotional books with memorable characters and compelling stories.

Connect with me on my website at BrendaGayle.com & sign up for *The Gayle Gazette,* my newsletter, to keep up-to-date on new releases, exclusive access to special features, giveaways, and all sorts of shenanigans

Until next time...

facebook.com/brendagaylebooks

ALSO BY BRENDA GAYLE

SEASONS OF LOVE

Twice & Forever - Autumn

Six Geese for Monica - Winter

The Color of You - Spring (coming February 2026)

The Parent Trip - Summer (coming May 2026)

Operation Soft Landing

(a military romantic suspense, coming Winter 2025/26)

HEART'S DESIRE ROMANTIC SUSPENSE

The Hungry Heart

The Doubting Heart

The Forsaken Heart

CHARLEY HALL HISTORICAL MYSTERIES

A Shot of Murder

Rigged for Murder

A Diagnosis of Murder

Odds on Murder

Murder in Abstract

Schooled in Murder

www.ingramcontent.com/pod-product-compliance
Lightning Source LLC
Chambersburg PA
CBHW020541080526
44583CB00013B/939